BLUE-COLLAR
CA$H

BLUE-COLLAR
CA$H

LOVE YOUR WORK, SECURE YOUR FUTURE, AND FIND HAPPINESS FOR LIFE

KEN RUSK

DEY ST.
An Imprint of WILLIAM MORROW

DEY ST.

HarperCollins books may be purchased for educational, business, or sales promotional use. For information, please email the Special Markets Department at SPsales@harpercollins.com.

FIRST EDITION

Designed by Renata De Oliveira

Illustrations on pages ii, viii, x, and chapter openers by Colorlife/Shutterstock

Library of Congress Cataloging-in-Publication Data has been applied for.

ISBN 978-0-06-298960-4

20 21 22 23 24 LSC 10 9 8 7 6 5 4 3 2 1

To my wife, Nancy, the girl in the blue-jean overalls I met so very long ago in our high school lunchroom. I'm so glad our birthdays are the same day, or who knows what would have happened. Thank you for so many things—for walking life's path with me, for weathering the occasional storm, for our wonderful daughter, Nicole, and for pushing me to write this book. All that I've accomplished, I've done with your support, your encouragement, and the joy I receive from your laughter and your smile.

CONTENTS

BLUE-COLLAR
CA$H

WHO ARE YOU AND WHY HAVE YOU COME TO THIS BOOK?

This may seem like an odd question to ask at the outset of a book you're already reading, but I can assure you, your answer will be one of the most important you've ever thought about. In fact, while you are thinking about that particular inquiry, let me throw a few more questions at you to help put you in the right frame of mind for what lies ahead in the coming chapters.

Whether you are nineteen or fifty, are you feeling frustrated living on the "hamster wheel" of just getting by or barely making ends meet? Making ends meet—what does that even mean, anyway? Maybe you are faced with the difficult choice of whether to pursue an expensive four-year degree or jump into a trade school and learn a much-needed skill. Are you a college graduate who has found the job market challenging? Or better yet, are you the parent of a college-age child who just isn't college material and you are wondering what he or she is going to make of him- or herself? Maybe you are thinking of changing your currently well-established career to do something you are truly passionate about but fear the uncertainty?

IF THE ANSWERS TO ANY OF THESE QUESTIONS IS YES, THEN READ ON—THIS BOOK is for you.

SO IF ANY OF THESE ARE YOU, LET ME JUST SAY THIS RIGHT FROM THE START: "CON-gratulations." I am thrilled for you! It looks like you're ready to make your *own* way. You're ready to follow your *own* path, a path that may or may not follow what society or your family or friends expect from you. What do I mean by that? Well, when we begin to think about what the rest of our lives are going to look like, many of us are faced with a multitude of options, which oftentimes can require difficult decisions. You might also call them choices. Life is a long series of choices we make on a daily basis. As mentioned earlier, one of them may be whether or not to pursue a higher education with its custom-ary mountain of debt. You know the drill: *Go to college. Take out school loans. Graduate. Get a forty-hour-a-week desk job. Work for corporate America. Try to climb the proverbial ladder.*

If the sound of this conventional path doesn't appeal much to you, then all I have to say is: *You may be right; it certainly didn't for me.* Yet no matter your current situation, today is the day you can begin to see what the rest of your life could become.

So now you've got this book in your hands, and it is going to help you see that the life you envision for yourself is certainly within reach. What kind of life? Well, I have given this some serious thought over many years, and I have come to the conclusion that a life of **comfort**, **peace**, and financial **freedom** is the ultimate goal. Not just one of those, but all three. I'll explain more on that a bit later, but suffice it to say for now that I'm going to be discussing these concepts, comfort, peace, and freedom, so often throughout this book that many times, they'll simply be abbreviated as "C, P, and F." This book is going to show you how to build a life that you get to design, build, and control . . . one that includes these three essential features. And best of all, it's going to show you how to create that life without necessarily having a fancy degree to get it done.

So many times on this journey of mine, I have been asked this question: Why are you writing this book? Well, there were times I wondered the same thing myself. And yet I quickly came to some very important answers, the most important of which is you. Yes, *you*. Because I AM you. I wrote this book for every person, young and old, who feels like they're not fully utilizing their talents, skills, and unique gifts. I wrote it for anyone who feels somewhere deep down inside that a conventional path just isn't the path for them, and that the typical corporate career isn't for them either. Perhaps you feel you'd be better off doing something you love but are reluctant to leave the safety of where you currently are. More important, this is a book that will help you see what is possible and help you define what it means to be successful—comfortable, peaceful, and financially free—and to accomplish that in a way that may now seem novel, but has been around for years. Ultimately, I wrote this book to give some clarity (and a little bit of hope) to those who might currently feel a bit left on the sidelines, looking in at the game and trying to figure out how they fit in.

My goal in each chapter is to help you realign your thinking in a way that will support you going forward. In each chapter, we will take a minute to help you improve how you look at the working world. Through real-life stories and some anecdotes I hope you find insightful, you will begin to see opportunities unfold right in front of you simply because you will learn to see things in a new and different light—a light that is solely intended to shine on you and you only. I want to show you—all of you—that it is still possible, maybe more possible than ever, to walk an unconventional path to success. In fact, as you can tell by the title, it is time to celebrate the possibilities, the opportunities, and the personal satisfaction that the blue-collar world can bring!

Careers that involve working with your hands, also known as blue-collar careers, are helping millions of people across the United States, and indeed around the globe, create rewarding, lucrative lives. *Remember this—I've always held the belief that we should plan our careers to support the vision of life we want for ourselves, not the other way around.*

So if you feel a bit stuck, and maybe a little confused about where your life is headed, or if you are desiring more momentum in your career and life, I want to assure you that there is a simple, clear way to break out of your current situation that will have you thinking outside the box. The blue-collar world is alive and well, and you can take full advantage of that, IF you are willing to work hard. Ever heard of Mike Rowe, the *Dirty Jobs* guy? He has built a whole career and personal brand out of celebrating the dignity, honor, and reward of hard work. And like Mike, I want you to begin to believe it is possible to plan and control your own life, your own purpose, your own future—regardless of the career path you choose. And I can help you create a path to finally achieve what YOU want out of this world.

If I had one wish here, if I could accomplish one thing, it would be that every person who is still on the fence about attending college or thinking about making a major change in their work lives, or even those who don't have a clue about what they want to do with the rest of their life, sees that there is so much more out there to be found. The job of your dreams is likely waiting for you to realize your true ambitions right now. I want you to know that success doesn't require a piece of framed piece of paper, wearing a suit, or toiling all day in some cubicle. . . . There is more than one path to success, and ultimately the freedom that comes with a well-planned and dedicated life. I wish everyone would stop sweating it. . . . The idea that you have to dig yourself into a hole financially in order to grow and flourish in a career is a scam. Now, you should know right from the beginning that I am NOT an anti-college guy. If you are going to manage other people's money, argue things in court, or operate on the human body, I would want you to know all there is to know to be effective, obviously. I am simply saying that college isn't for everybody; it never has been. And for those finding themselves wondering how they can get their lives going the way THEY want them to go, rest assured this book will show you how to be confident and calm and cool—blue-collar cool—knowing that there is a path out there for you, where you can earn without the college burden. So this story is for you—you dreamers, you risk takers, you faithful listeners of your inner voice—who trust and know that you deserve a life that is comfortable, peaceful, and free.

Throughout the book I will share not only my own personal and professional story, but also the success stories of countless other inspiring individuals who have followed their own unique paths to discover lives of comfort, peace, and freedom. You will read about some interesting people and learn about their outlook on the lost art of hard work. Interestingly, these individuals all have certain characteristics in common that have made them successful—characteristics such as **vision**, **faith**, **courage**, **initiative**, **humility**, **resilience**, **persistence**, **simplicity**, and **generosity**. I am honored to share their stories with you to help illustrate how they used these traits to help them along their paths to success. I am honored to call them colleagues, friends, and family. Upon learning about their individual journeys, some fraught with serious challenges, I am certain you will come to your own conclusion that you have more control over your life, and most things in it, than you might currently think.

Now, I have some exciting news for you, and it is this: what you should know right from the start is that each of you possesses these same nine critical characteristics for success—you really do! They are inside each and every one of us. And I will help you bring them out. You might say that you already have them in your closet, you just haven't worn them yet. You simply need a reason to, and this book will give you that.

A study done by Andrea J. Stenberg of The Baby Boomer Entrepreneur* has shown that in order to internalize a new concept or idea, meaning to integrate it into your values, beliefs, and identity, you must hear it or see it a minimum of seven

---

* Andrea J. Stenberg, "What Is the Rule of Seven? And How Will It Improve Your Marketing?" The Baby Boomer Entrepreneur, December 7, 2015, https://www .thebabyboomerentrepreneur.com/258/what-is-the-rule-of-seven-and-how-will-it -improve-your-marketing.

times. With that in mind, you will notice we have **bolded** those words when they are discussed in order to help you truly own them.

Now, if I am successful, by the time you've finished reading this book you will have realized that though there are many paths to your own success, there is indeed a path that is uniquely for *you*. If you can unlock what's in your own heart and mind and use this information to help build your own virtual path, and then set out to follow it, you can control your destiny. I believe that there is nothing more powerful in the world than the individual's ability to visualize—and then create—one's own life. And that is what I will teach you how to do in this book. Once you realize that you possess the power, and use it responsibly, nothing is impossible. Remember these two things as you read along: (1) I believe everyone has the ability to be the person they were meant to be and (2) No one is in charge of your success—your comfort, peace, and freedom—except for you. So let's dig in and get started.

1

THE POWER OF YOUR MIND: HOW DO YOU SEE YOURSELF?

My first goal is for you to try to change the way you see your life and your future. I'd like you to begin by focusing on exactly how you see yourself one, three, five, ten, and twenty years from now . . . or at least to the point of your soon-to-be clearly envisioned life of comfort, peace, and freedom. Before I can ask you to think differently about how you might spend your future vocational days, you must first begin with that picture clearly imprinted in your mind's eye. Ask yourself this question: Have you ever backed your car out of the driveway, put the shifter into drive, about to step on the gas, and had absolutely no idea of where it is you planned on going? I sincerely hope the answer to that question is a hard no! But regardless, that shouldn't be the way you view your longer-term future. This is the first step in changing the way you look at the next few decades.

In this chapter, we will take a close look at how you think about the balance of life and work. We will take stock of how much we prioritize both of these two concepts. And just maybe while we're at it, we should examine how much control each one might have over the other (and over you). The funny thing here is that I have learned that many of us have a very consistent current behavior . . . and we might not even know it.

One of the most important questions you can ask yourself is: How do I see *myself*? Better yet, how would I describe *myself* to someone else? Stay with me here. I have had the honor of getting some pretty good advice over the years, some of which I will share with you now. It's pretty simple, and you may have heard it before. It goes like this: "People shouldn't live to work; they should work to live."

Let's think about that for a moment. Can you grasp the concept that maybe, just maybe it isn't so much *what* you do for a living, but what you do *with* what you do for a living that matters? Allow that to sink in for a bit . . . and give me a long leash here. Remember, I am a blue-collar guy and have been since I was fifteen years old. And one of my goals is to get you to think differently about blue-collar work and all the opportunities that it can bring, especially today as fewer and fewer of us have the knowledge, the desire, or, most important, the ability to work in that world. In 1986, I started with six employees. Now, thirty-two years later, we employ over two hundred. During that time, I have interviewed and hired thousands of people to become part of our construction business. It's a pretty tough gig—we dig a lot of ditches; we use jackhammers and buckets of tar and concrete and dump trucks full of gravel. It's not for everyone, and I am keenly aware of that fact when I look for new employees. And in light of those facts, I always begin each interview with a simple question: "Why are you here?"

I almost always get the same answer: "I need a job."

"Okay, but why are you here?" I continue.

"I need to make money," they say.

"Okay, money for what?" I ask.

"Well, I've got bills to pay," they answer.

"Bills for what?" I inquire.

"Well, I want to get caught up, maybe get ahead," they respond.

I continue to push. "What does getting ahead look like to you?"

"Well, I'd like to get a new _____ and then improve my _____ and then move into a _____."

"Aha! Now we are getting somewhere!" I tell them.

Now we'll all get somewhere in the next section.

VISION—THE ABILITY TO THINK ABOUT YOUR FUTURE WITH IMAGINATION AND WISDOM

As you can see, my goal is to take an individual from thinking about this Friday (and every Friday, for that matter) and get them to start thinking about their life from a long-term perspective. Now here's the fun part. It all begins with a box of Crayola crayons. You'll be hearing more about my "crayon therapy" in a bit. I came to this simple yet enormously effective exercise about thirty years ago as I was sitting in my office one day. It was an accident at the time, but soon it turned into a practice that I have firmly entrenched into our company's day. Why? Because it works. Let me give you a great example.

I get asked all the time about the secret to living the life you have always dreamed of. Well, my answer is always the same. Define a dream. What exactly is a dream? Merriam-Webster's dictionary says it is "a series of visions, images, thoughts or aspirations that can occur while you are awake or asleep." Look closely at those words: **IMAGES** and **VISIONS**. In other words, a dream is something you SEE. You focus on what you desire most, and your subconscious takes over and creates images in your mind, reflecting the life you want. Hence the title of this chapter.

If you are unsure about what it is you want to do in life or where your talents lie, take heart. **Vision**, I assure you, is not gifted at birth. It takes *practice*. Anyone can learn how to create goals and envision their future. But while we all possess the ability to become visionaries, some of us tend to be better at envisioning our future than others. Have you ever met someone who bought an old, dilapidated house and said, "Just look at the bones of this place! They're awesome. Can't you just see the potential?" while all you can imagine was the asbestos hanging from the ceiling and mice scurrying across the floor? Your friend had what we call *vision*. They could look beyond their present circumstances and clearly see the *possible*, what *could* be done in the future.

You don't need a college degree to be a visionary, and you don't have to be psychic or a Zen master either. You need to start making goals, goals that you can clearly visualize, the kind of goals that you wake up thinking about. They don't have to be impossible goals. Start small. This is a learning/doing process. Soon enough, you'll be amazed at what you can achieve.

One of my first examples of this process comes from the experiences of one of my own employees. Remember when I said I started thirty-two years ago with just six employees?

Well, one of them was a young man named Tim Despoth. I met Tim in 1988 when I was sitting in my eight-by-ten closet, I mean office. Tim was just twenty years old at the time. He was a big guy with an intimidating presence, but he was willing to work and eager to learn. Though he had come from a supportive family, he wanted to build his own life for himself and see what he could accomplish. I really admired that.

Tim was a guy I could relate to, as he and I had some things in common—some good things and some not so good, actually. Both of us were relatively new to our positions, neither of us had gone to college, and oddly enough, we even shared some facial scars from early childhood. Mine were caused by a birth defect called a cleft palate and the subsequent surgeries, and his by a tragic backyard accident. He had endured a half-dozen surgeries to repair some horrible burns he had suffered from a bonfire while horse-playing with his brothers and a mishandled jar of lantern fuel.

Despite our shared tragedies, both Tim and I seemed quite capable of laughing about it, and laugh we did. However, one day Tim came to me, and the minute he walked into my office I knew we weren't going to be laughing. Tim made it clear with his expression that this was to be a serious conversation. He was struggling to keep his world straight, he told me. His young wife had a serious long-term recovery from a recent intestinal surgery, and the medical bills were piling up. He found himself in several thousand dollars of debt, with no way out. Here was this big, strong guy with his head in his hands. "I just don't know what to do," he said quietly. Now, Tim is normally the kind of guy who just keeps to himself and wants his private life to stay that way, so this was a turning point—for him, for me, for our relationship.

Back then, I was admittedly buried in my own issues. At work in a new and young company, I was in survival mode most of the time. The thought of planning ahead was the furthest thing from my mind. It was the day-to-day battles of customers, building inspectors, banks, bill collectors, and so on that occupied most of my brain and left little room for the type of creative thinking I needed at that moment. My bucket was full.

But on this day, Tim and I forged ahead. We sat together for the rest of the day and wondered aloud about what we could do to get him out of his predicament. We thought long and hard about a plan to get rid of his debt and get him back on track, thereby avoiding just giving up and throwing in the towel. No, that was NOT an option for this guy. There was no doubt that whatever path we figured out, he would battle his way through it like a platoon leader taking a hill. I often remember him saying, "I am willing to work really hard to get where I want to be, so help me figure out what I need to do and I promise you I'll get it done." From that moment on, Tim had a clear **vision**. He wanted a life that was debt-free. He wanted to be released from the burdens those debts were having on his quality of life.

And with that, we went for it. We started with a dream—Tim's dream. We talked about looking way beyond the medical bills, as that was a temporary problem, albeit a daunting one for him. We wanted to think big, real big. We started drawing, just doodling at first. You know, a pen and some crude images on a piece of scrap paper. What were his dreams, his aspirations, his images? He mentioned to me that his dream was to buy a new pickup truck. His father had worked at a GM transmission plant and always had a new vehicle to drive.

All right, that's good, but let's go further, I thought. We talked about how someday (remember that word; we're gonna redefine it in a bit) he would like to buy some land and build a house for the family he and his wife were planning. Wow, that was a pretty good goal for a twenty-year-old to put out there. Talk about beginning with the end in mind, another concept we'll take a deep dive into in a later chapter.

Now, as much as I wanted Tim to focus on the big thinking, we had to solve some immediate problems first, most notably the medical bills. Within an hour or so, we had a plan to pay them off. Sure, it would take a couple years and all the extra bonus money he could scrape together, but soon that problem was in the rearview mirror. He put away a little money each week, made a deal with the hospital to take payments, and had a completion date for paying off the debt. First, he had the **vision**, then he **made** the **plan**, then he **worked** the plan. And before he knew it, he was on his path to success. Two years later, when he finished paying off his medical debt, he felt more confident. He thought about his next goal. He thought of the vehicle. As I said earlier, he had always had his eye on a brand-new GMC pickup truck—a big, shiny, black, badass truck. It was a perfect match for him, seeing he was 6'3" and about 240 pounds. And so there we went again. He needed to save for a down payment. He set up a weekly withdrawal and set his sights on a completion date. It was a tough row to hoe, but soon, after forty weeks of saving fifty bucks per week, he was in the dealership picking out his new ride. Talk about a big moment. You should have seen him the day he rolled that truck into the parking lot for the first time. The other foremen just stood and stared in disbelief. One of them actually said, "Man, you are so lucky!" Wrong thing to say to a guy who just spent the better part of five years bustin' his ass to dig himself out from the weight of all that undeserved debt, and yet still found a way to save for a new truck.

"It ain't luck, pal," he said. "I earned this baby." What Tim was really saying is this: All of this worked out for him because we were able to SEE it working, beginning to end. We had a clear path to walk, and walk it we did.

Now with two **visions** and **plans** executed, Tim was a goal-oriented machine. And that was a good thing because he and his wife, Mary, were building quite the bench of a future football team—four boys in total—and he needed a place to house them all. A home was now as much a necessity as it was a goal. Now Tim had a new **vision**—a home and some land for his growing family. Within weeks, he had identified a five-acre plot out in the country. It had tall pine trees, plenty of open space for a pond, and a great spot to put up a house. Again, he designed a path to keep his dream alive and moving. The lot would cost him plenty, so this was a task he had to take seriously.

But a funny thing happened as Tim articulated his dreams and created plans to achieve them. Tim had now been with our company just over five years. During that time, he had become an effective crew chief, then foreman, then field supervisor. Turns out that becoming a goal-driven person reflects in all your walks of life, not only personally but also socially and professionally. So it was no surprise to see Tim grab promotion after promotion, using his learned skills to move up, and fast. In what seemed like no time at all, he was running our entire production department.

Three years later, and only eight years into his tenure with our company, Tim broke ground on his new home. He would visit the site often, four boys in tow, inspecting anything newly done that day by the contractors. Funny how a new door handle, or a sink faucet, or even a window, can be so exciting as you watch your dream slowly rise out of the ground right before your eyes. A prouder father and husband you couldn't find. Tim and Mary would experience much comfort raising those boys in that home. That was twenty years ago, and since then he has spent that time paying down the mortgage and saving for the future. Today, Tim enjoys a debt-free life, building their retirement, saving all the money he can while watching one boy after another graduate from college and start their own lives—all working for my ditch-digging company, mind you.

Of course, being who he is, he isn't stopping now. Just the other day I saw him putting a new dream on our company's goals board. His children are grown, so now he and Mary are thinking of the next phase in their lives. The home where they have raised those four young men no longer fits their needs. So off he goes again. He has a plan to build their retirement home. I for one can't wait to see that vision become a reality too.

Tim's story was an inspiration for this book. The day he walked into my office was the day I first helped someone envision and realize their dreams. Tim already possessed the character trait of **vision**. He just needed practice executing it, and as we all know by now, with enough practice at anything, you can become a master of it. Tim is, indeed, a master visionary. And soon you will be too!

THE FIVE-GALLON-BUCKET HEAD

In my ditch-digging business, we use five-gallon buckets—a lot of them. We use them to haul dirt, chunks of broken concrete, and other construction debris out of the basements and crawl spaces we repair. We typically go through at least three to four hundred buckets per season, and they are like gold to our crews. You find them fifteen to twenty relatively new buckets with solid, clean handles, and they react like you just bought them an expensive lunch. Yes, we have an odd but well-earned affinity for these buckets, and not too long ago I started thinking. Working with these guys over the years and watching them fill these buckets, I began to wonder about our minds and how they can fill up so quickly with thoughts, some of which can actually impede our ability to think clearly about our future. And so it's no surprise that I came to see that the human psyche is strangely similar to a five-gallon bucket.

I believe that our brains have capacities, just like a five-gallon bucket. I know that sounds crazy, and I certainly don't have any medical studies to back this up, but I am taking theoretical license here, so just listen to me for a moment. I'll try to make some sense of this for you.

I believe that the first and second gallons in our buckets, or brains, are used for the basics of living. Let's say they're reserved for the heavy work of keeping us alive—creating our DNA, cell division and development, building strong bones, repairing muscles, creating antibodies and white blood cells for attacking unwanted intruders. Additionally, these two primary gallons support our red blood cell counterparts to deliver much-needed nutrients to maintain our autonomic processes—such as breathing and keeping our hearts beating. Most of these amazing actions take place without any outward sign or signal of their occurrence. Thankfully, these actions require no thinking whatsoever. However, if something goes wrong—medically—with these buckets, the rest pretty much falls to pieces.

Gallon three is charged with things like movement, positioning, and protection and survival. This includes walking around, grasping things, keeping clear space from objects and others in our paths, using our inner GPS system, shielding ourselves from the elements, recognizing and nourishing our bodies from hunger and thirst, lifting things, using tools, motor skills—you get the idea.

Gallon four is where it starts to get interesting, because this is the space we use to fill our brains with information. It's all the stuff we eventually learn, mostly by choice. It's the input that goes into our brains' blank hard drive. When we're born, it's the space we use to learn shapes and numbers, to read and write, to add and subtract, and to reason and create. In other words, we learn skills that we can use later in life. Yes, gallon four is an amazing place: an organized, methodical, process-oriented place that has no boundaries, no limits, and most important, no competition from any of the other buckets.

Gallon five. This is where it gets kind of tricky. This is the gallon where our emotions hang out. As emotions go, some are positive (light) and some are negative (heavy). This a busy place as these emotions are always coming and going quickly. And let me just say, if you want to be able to hold your head high, stay positive, and keep focused on the task at hand, this gallon needs to be kept light, positive, and full of supportive energy. It needs to be kept neat and tidy and relatively open. Your bucket is already heavy. Four of the five gallons always remain mostly full. If you fill this last gallon with heavier emotions—anger, jealousy, stress, fear, frustration, and disappointment, you will have no space for excitement, spontaneity, confidence, happiness, desire, love, comfort, peace, and freedom.

Easier said than done, right?

Gallon five is the last gallon to be filled; it's a surface gallon. You can see it, and usually everyone else can too. It's by far the most noticeably active region in the bucket of your brain. Because there's no lid to our bucket, we think we can just keep filling and filling this gallon with all sorts of emotions. And emotions are nothing more than your body's reactions to outside events, or your perception of those events. They are like an unruly child. You never know from minute to minute what you are going to get. But there is another, even larger problem with gallon number five. Our buckets simply can't hold all our emotions at the same time. Our brains only have so much room. Something has got to give, so we constantly make decisions about what we let in and what we reject.

There is often an ongoing struggle between two sets of emotions: the one set that is already there, and the others trying to get in. As I said earlier, these two sets, positive emotions and negative emotions, are very powerful and in many cases are engaged in this constant turf battle. There is no room for both these groups. It's one or the other. Stressing out over a bill kicks out a spontaneous neighborhood walk with your kids. Feeling like a failure at work kicks out the confidence of making a good score at the Saturday-morning golf game. The self-inflicted feeling of jealousy toward your coworker gives the boot to feeling the need to volunteer at church. Fear of a deadline overrides telling someone close that you love and appreciate them. People don't realize that these emotions are not involuntary. They are actually quite voluntary. Believe it or not, they are a *choice*. Think about that. You are constantly making split-second choices about how you emotionally react to various events. . . .

You and you alone *choose* what to put in your five-gallon

bucket. If you choose to let in a negative emotion, you must kick out a positive one. Just try it. Now add in several negative emotions. You'll find you have no room left for the positive ones, the ones you'd like to see in yourself, the ones you'd like others to see in you. Next time you are in a negative funk, simply ask yourself this one question out loud: "Is this where I choose to be right now? Are these the emotions I am choosing to let in?"

In short, our brains can only handle so much. Put too much in there, it's too heavy. You can't carry it all. It will most definitely overflow. But if you fill it just right, it does the work for you. I came to this theory after observing two different approaches to the same work challenge by two of our company's installers. One day I asked two of my crew foremen to work a little longer to finish a job with the promise of a three-day weekend to follow. The first foreman was excited, happy to take the work on, and grateful for the three-day weekend. The second foreman—not so much. He was angry, resentful, and not happy at all about the pressure or the work.

Hmmmm, I thought. I needed to understand this. I paid both men the same salary and require both men to do the same work, but their attitudes and approaches to that work were entirely different. The more I observed and got to know each man, the more I realized what was going on. The "positive" foreman had more reserve in his tank; the five-gallon bucket of his head wasn't filled all the way to the brim. He had room to absorb new information. The "negative" foreman was tapped out. His head was full. He had worries, problems, anxieties, stresses, and there was no space for flexibility in that head of his.

He couldn't see the three-day weekend ahead of him. He literally had no space to see it. But here's the thing. That's no excuse. At any point in time, he is the one in charge of filling his bucket. He's the one who can cap it off at a certain point. He's the one who can choose to see the good and positive outcomes of his labor.

Yes, you heard that right. Anger is a choice, a choice you consciously make. Jealousy is a choice. Resentment is a choice. Feeling hopeless is a choice. Feeling that your life isn't what you hoped or expected it to be is a choice. You are actually choosing the emotions you want to let in, the ones that fill up that most important fifth gallon. And once you realize that, you can change immediately. Yes, you might still have that nagging Visa bill, or that temporary setback, or even that crazy coworker. But with a little planning and some clear-cut paths in your life, you'll soon realize that you are, in fact, in control of your emotions. *You* can *choose* to love the work you do and find the good in it. *You* can also choose to stick to it and not think your life would be so much better if you had done something different. Deciding to be happy on your path in life will ultimately determine your happiness level. It doesn't work the other way around. If you spend your life waiting for a certain career breakthrough or a windfall of cash, you'll never be happy. Choosing happiness, positivity, and a mind-set that is open to new opportunities *is* the path—to comfort and peace and freedom.

GET OUT A BOX OF SIXTY-FOUR CRAYOLA CRAYONS

To close this chapter, I am going to ask you to perform a small exercise, an exercise in visualization, which I know is going to change your life. You will need to have as clear of a mind as you can muster. You will need to be open-minded as to the possibilities of your future. I hear that all the time—"Let's be open-minded about this idea." Ever wonder what "open-minded" actually means? I did, so once again I researched it, as I enjoy defining terms that folks have used over and over for years, sometimes not knowing what they truly mean or in which circumstances they are intended. In this case, the definition I like best is this: having an open mind means having the room or space for new thoughts to settle into. Most of us are guilty of letting too much into our brains so that new ideas have no room to seed and grow. For right now, it's time to clear out that fifth gallon completely; I'll need you to be as creative as possible. So take some quiet time, breathe deeply, and allow that emotion-filled gallon to just pour out. . . . Ready?

Now, you probably haven't had a crayon in your hand in a very long time, at least since you were a child, and that's fine. However, you are about to embark on a journey. A journey of your own creation. And you will be doing this by experiencing two extremes, one being your ability to take many steps toward looking ahead, by going back in time, back to the time when you first learned color, to draw, and to "keep it in the lines." This is a serious thing. If you really want to create a life that YOU want for yourself, a life that lets you be you, one that is comfortable, peaceful, and free, then this is an amazing but crucial first step. Where am I going with this? It's really quite simple. This is an exercise I have been doing with my staff for many years now, and one that is not only fun to do, but enormously eye-opening for the participant. If done correctly, you will learn a lot about your ability to visualize into the future. Again, anyone can do this, and, I submit, all of us should. So here we go.

- You'll need a few everyday items to get started. Most of these probably exist in your home already.
- You'll need a large piece of white paper, the bigger the better. Poster board is great.
- You'll also need a box of crayons. Seriously, find a box of crayons, the more colors the better (my fave is the sixty-four box of Crayola crayons—lots of great shades in there).
- Now find a quiet space to think, dream, and visualize. Let's plan on at least an hour, just to get started. Ready? Here we go.
- Just a note here—this is one of those times when you should be as selfish as possible. This is YOUR life plan being painted on a canvas for you to have and review as you proceed along the path to its successful completion. So think *ME* right now. What does your vision or version of C, P, and F look like?
- Begin by asking yourself this extremely important and life-changing question: *What exactly do I want my life to look like?*
- Now take time to have some fun. Take out your paper and your crayons and lose yourself for a while. Begin by drawing just anything that comes to mind. Start small, by drawing the best version of yourself. How do you want to look and feel? How do you want to be seen?
- Now expand that a bit. What type of relationship do you see yourself in? Do you see yourself as married or single, with kids or without? How many? Draw it as best as you can.
- Next, ask yourself what type of living quarters you see yourself in—a farmhouse in the country, a condo near

a lake, a house in the suburbs, or an apartment in the city? Go ahead and draw your dream home in the most colorful, vivid detail you can envision.

- Now, about your personal transportation: Are you a car person or a minivan, SUV, or pickup truck person, or maybe even a motorcycle or an electric city scooter type? Have fun here—draw it as clearly as you can. Choose the color, make, and model.

- Let's keep going with our drawing. Are you a pet person, and if so, do you see a dog or a cat, and if so, exactly what kind or breed? Draw it as clearly as you can. Don't worry about your drawing ability.

- Now ask yourself about your hobbies. Are you a kayaker, a golfer, a jogger, a yoga enthusiast, or a gardener? One of your goals is time and financial freedom, so what will you do with your time? Draw it. I know this can be difficult, so get it done in small pieces at a time.

- Leave it and come back to it. I cannot stress enough: take your time here! This is no different from a jigsaw puzzle that you leave out on the table so you can slowly but surely complete it one piece at a time. Take the time and get it right, as you are literally drawing your life here. It's not the quantity of things you draw into your life plan, it's the quality of your eventual life that you are visualizing. This is really high-impact stuff we're doing here!

NOW, IN THE NEXT FEW CHAPTERS, WE'RE GOING TO DISCUSS THE CURRENT STATE of the American workforce and how you can take unbeliev-

able advantage of today's reality to support your life plan. Your
Crayola crayon plan. You will need that drawing and the ability
to keep an open mind (fifth gallon) with this information as it
relates to matching *your* potential with the opportunities. You
will want to have that clear **vision** of what you want your life
to look like. In other words, if you can't SEE your life in clear,
colorful, and vivid detail . . . you will have a seriously tough
time achieving it. But there is good news! You see, the way our
brains work is a wonderfully powerful thing. And if you can
begin to draw a clear picture of how you see yourself and the
world you want to create, and keep that in front of you, you will
most *certainly* obtain all that you seek.

A recent study by Professor Dave Kohl at Virginia Tech[*]
shows how many of us could benefit from receiving, and then
later referencing, our goals. Professor Kohl found that 80 percent of us admit to not having any real goals. Of the remaining
20 percent, he found that 16 percent do have goals but fail to
document them. Of the last 4 percent, Professor Kohl found
that three out of four people write down their goals but then fail
to review them regularly. And finally, just 1 percent of those in
this group choose to not only record their goals in great detail
but also keep them out in the open, reviewing their progress
regularly. Oh, and one final discovery: those in the 1 percent
are likely to earn nine times more money during their lifetimes
than the 80 percent.

Good luck with your drawings. It's a fun exercise, one that
I have seen in action countless times. In fact, one of my favorite things to do at my company is to review the life plans of

---

[*] *Dixie Gillaspie, "You'll Never Accomplish Goals You Don't Really Care About,"*
Entrepreneur, *January 20, 2017, https://www.entrepreneur.com/article/254371.*

my employees, check on their progress toward their goals, celebrate their wins, and then get busy setting the next one. So get out your crayons and get in the game! Start seeing your world the way YOU want it. In this author's opinion, there is no better way to lead a fulfilling and rewarding life.

As we move forward, there is one additional piece to the overall success of your new Crayola world vision. Take some time to think about the answer to this question: What if I were to ask you about what you might choose to do if you were to take on a blue-collar job? Really think carefully about this. You can choose whatever you want to do, whatever you might be good at or passionate about. When you are done, we will pair that up with what you want your life to look like—what you drew on your life picture. And with those two important pieces to our life puzzle in hand, we'll start walking that path.

To close this chapter, here's a quick formula I'd like you to remember:

Vocational Passion + Life Vision = a Comfortable, Peaceful, and Financially Free Life. **Comfort**, **peace**, and **freedom**—you'll hear me mention these three words many times. Maybe you'd like to know what they mean and how I came up with them as my personal meaning of life, my personal mantra, if you will. In the next chapter, we will explore exactly that—my meaning of life, and how you can accomplish it for yourself, regardless of your education level or choice of occupation. Interested? Then read on.

2

MY STORY

So I should probably take a minute to tell you a little bit about myself. For those who know me well, they'll tell you this is something I am not always comfortable doing. But I hope that by sharing some of the early challenges I had in my life, and how I was able to take them on, I can help others look their own problems in the face and say enough is enough. And while we're doing that, it is my goal that together, we can get in touch with what might be the most important obstacles in your life as well.

I myself took a path that didn't involve college, and through hard work and always being on the lookout for better opportunities, I wound up being a successful and happy guy. I am able to provide a great life for my family, not to mention satisfy some of the big-kid things in life that I've always wanted, like fast cars and international travel. I know from my own expe-

rience, first as a day laborer digging ditches and then eventually as the owner of a successful waterproofing company, that
working with your hands at a job that takes skill and practice
can be not only monumentally rewarding but life-affirming as
well.

To be honest, as someone who grew up in this world being judged, looked down upon, and in some cases downright
ridiculed, I have empathy for others who are desperately trying
to hold their heads up high and choose a unique path for themselves. It's not easy to stand up to others, let alone an entire
system.

You see, I was born with a birth defect, a facial deformity
known as a cleft palate. It occurs when the roof of the mouth
doesn't fuse properly and leaves a large gap, basically a hole
from the upper lip all the way to the back of the throat. As a
young child, I endured barbaric maxillofacial surgeries to repair this condition, some of which included bone grafts to the
nose and the roof of my mouth to create normal function. The
surgeries and the recoveries were painful, but not quite as painful as being bullied by other children. As we all know, kids can
be *brutal*. I remember with startling clarity a time during the
second grade when I was so ashamed of the severe rashes and
painful scabs all over my mouth and nose from my surgeries,
I hid my face behind a folder just to walk between classes. All
I wanted was to get to the next class, sit in my chair, keep my
head down, and do my work—*without* being made fun of by
my peers. But the insults came, and always from the same few
sources. They were terrible, both the insults *and* the bullies.

Needless to say, I developed some serious insecurities. But
as will become apparent shortly, I also developed serious empathy, not to mention a few other skill sets that have served

me well. I think they can also help you. I truly believe we all have our own "deformities" that we are constantly aware of or working to overcome. And many times, they might not be as obvious as mine. In fact, some of you may be carrying the burden of something that can't even be seen. Anxiety, fear, disapproval, going against seemingly good advice—these are just some of the things that can paralyze us from seeing who we can truly be.

Looking back, I can remember how I discovered the power of humor, self-deprecation, humility, risk-taking, trust, and listening to my own inner voice. I learned these powers, funnily enough, by implementing them all at once. I clearly remember those days in junior high and how one of the schoolyard bullies just loved to throw these rather nasty verbal shots at my appearance. You see, I was a skinny twelve-year-old kid, no more than half his weight, who had no chance of holding my own physically against the meathead who had lobbed the insult. And so I made the hasty decision to use my wits instead. When the bully attempted to show off in front of the girls by yelling that I looked like a "monster," I shocked him and the girls I was standing with by *agreeing* with him. Waving my arms in the air crazily and making a scary face, I groaned, "You know what? You're right! I am a scary monster!" Using self-deprecation, humor, and the element of surprise, I took my nemesis off guard. The shock of having his own insult used against him froze him in his tracks. The girls standing around me laughed, which defused what could have been a hostile situation.

Not being ashamed of who you are—and that goes for what you think, what you believe, where you live, what you enjoy doing, where you work, and how you make a living—is one of the most important traits you can have as a human being. I took a risk by speaking up, all the while knowing I could have been pummeled by the much bigger, meaner boy. I did what I did because the alternative—continuing to be bullied and put down—was not an option for me. I had to have trust in myself. I had to believe I could change the situation and take control of my own life. I had to listen to the voice inside me that said: *You deserve better than this, Ken.*

The skills I developed at the tender age of twelve, or rather *realized* I already had within me all along, are every bit as relevant today—not just to my life but to yours as well. You don't have to feel trapped into thinking that you must fit into some mold to be successful, or into a life *others* deem beautiful, good, smart, worthy, or whole. Societal norms, the proverbial "bullies" of our daily existence, don't have to determine your future or, more important, how you view yourself. You don't have to let what others think determine what you're supposed to look like, sound like, work like, live like, or *be* like. I am sure glad *I* didn't. The skinny little kid with a bent nose, scarred lip, and bad teeth could have retreated into a dark corner somewhere and felt sorry for himself, but he didn't, and you don't have to either. You can learn to trust yourself—trust your inner voice, trust that everything will work out, if you're willing to take risks and try something new, perhaps travel a different path in life that others might not have the courage to take—or to advise. Having a positive mind-set (a sense of humor doesn't hurt either), a work ethic, and a willingness to control your own destiny is all that is required. Once you're prepared to stand up and take charge of your life, and this goes for anyone regardless of your age, then you're prepared to find what path will make you the best *you* that *you* can be.

Remember earlier on when we discussed choices? I learned at a young age that everyone has a choice in life—and we make a thousand of them every day. They all add up. Every moment of every day, you have the choice to be the victim in the school-yard of life, or you can stand up and say: *Enough! I want and deserve more.*

One of the biggest choices you'll ever make is choosing your career. It will determine a number of other viable paths. Deciding who you are, what you enjoy doing, how you want to spend the hours of your day, what kind of lifestyle you feel will make you happy, and then following a path that leads you in that direction, is imperative to living a comfortable, peace-ful, and freedom-filled life. But to do this, you need to listen to the voice inside you. You need to know your limitations as well as your talents. Understanding how to work with, sometimes around, your own "deformity" is up to you and no one else.

MY STORY

As for my early career, I had no idea I would end up as a ditch digger, let alone a happy and successful one. For nearly thirty years, I've been digging my way to a good life, one shovel of dirt at a time, and teaching others to do the same. When I was starting out, I was a lot like you. I didn't have a clue about what I wanted to do with my life, and I wasn't quite sure what path to take to get me to where I was supposed to go—to adulthood, a career, a family, a life. Like most teenagers in those days, I tried several jobs just to make some money. I scrubbed floors in a small-town bakery, delivered newspapers (hated that), emp-tied ashtrays at a bowling alley, caddied at a local golf course, even detailed cars for my father's friends. All the while, I was going to high school knowing one day I would be considering a degree because that's what you're supposed to do. Back in the seventies, though, college wasn't pushcd as hard as it is now, and with good reason. One could say I was lucky in that regard. I recall one day sitting in my economics class when the teacher asked us to raise our hands if we planned on attending college. Only a third of us raised our hands. The rest planned to do what our parents did: work and earn money to support ourselves. We didn't overthink it, and our peers, parents, and society didn't look down upon us for choosing that path. It was that attitude, a popular one at the time, that pointed me toward an opportunity that was literally right under my nose.

Back then, a fence separated the south side of my high school from a local foundation waterproofing company. To get to and from school, I used to walk through a hole in the fence, and I would pass by the building. Every day I saw a bustling business—people coming in and out—and one day I decided to check it out for myself. My brother, who was four years older than I was, had started working there during high school, and I figured I could do the same. To this day, I remember the energy and excitement I felt when I walked through those doors. Salespeople were walking up and down the halls making deals. Supervisors were barking orders across the room; others were headed out to job sites. I walked right in and asked what I could do for work. One of the guys in the office asked if I had ever used a shovel or run a jackhammer or even spent any time in an office. I told him I was willing to give anything a shot. I did, and I never looked back.

I started my first full-time career working around foundations to waterproof homes. In the thirty years since, I've worked in every aspect of the business. In the beginning, I dug ditches every summer and made sales calls during the winter.

I clocked a few thousand hours on the line digging before I was eventually promoted. I kept my eye on the available opportunities, which led to working in the warehouse, supplying crews with their materials. I then moved into the front office, where I joined the marketing team helping to sell our products and services. Soon I was involved in order financing, going to the homes of our customers to get their bank loan paperwork squared away. As the years went by, I ended up doing every job available in the building. I eventually learned how to run an entire business. This was where some tough choices had to be made. Choices that would change my life forever.

At this point, the growth of the company dictated that we create a franchise program so we could expand across the Midwest. I remember the owner coming to my brother and me and saying, "Guys, we need to grow this thing. I want you to create a franchise program and start opening offices."

That was how he did things back then. The boss would just drop a huge task in your lap and say, "Make it happen!" I remember sitting there afterward and saying to my brother, "Well, never done this before. How we gonna do it?" But we took it on, built the program, began marketing it, and soon we had a half dozen or so candidates who wanted to give it a shot.

Here's where the choices came in. You see, while this was developing, I had only recently enrolled in college. Not because I wanted to, but because I thought I *had* to. So there I was, at somewhat of a crossroads. Stay in school, pursuing a nonspecific business degree, or travel the Midwest, opening offices for a company that I knew very well?

After a long talk with my father, a successful businessman without a college degree himself, my decision was made. I remember my dad saying, "Well, Ken, the easiest thing for me to say right now is to stay in school and get your degree. However, I know of no better way to learn business than to open offices for someone else, getting paid to learn how to do it, and making mistakes with someone else's money. You're not going to find that in any college." That was all I needed to hear. I took the position and dropped out of school.

For the next four years, I was mostly on the road, opening offices across Ohio, Indiana, and Illinois. On Sunday nights, I would hug Nancy goodbye, get in my car, and travel to the latest new location, trying to get the fledgling company to stand on its own two feet. Living out of a suitcase, sleeping in cheap hotels, and eating unhealthy food took its toll. Don't get me wrong, I loved the knowledge and experience I was gaining in the process, but I knew that this was a stepping-stone to bigger things. I still had that picture of my desired life firmly imprinted in my mind, and in order to get it, I knew I had to grow even more.

And then another opportunity presented itself. In 1986, I decided it was time. My brother and I met with the owner of the foundation repair company where we had been working and told him that we were ready to take the next step. The only remaining franchise location available in Ohio was in the west end of the state, in Toledo. So we begged the bank for a small credit line, packed up our stuff, and moved our families to our new location, and our new life.

After several years of sixty- to seventy-hour weeks, we had built a successful business. And then another and another. Eventually, I became president. I went from digging the trenches to becoming the boss of a few hundred employees. And it doesn't end there. I still had to have goals even after I had reached the pinnacle of my career. I had to continue to live a life of anticipation. My goal was to create multiple lines of income in order to insulate myself from any one sector downturn, to avoid "putting all my eggs in one basket," as the old saying goes. I kept my eyes open for opportunities, which led to one investment after another, and made those additional incomes a reality.

Today, my portfolio is diverse and cuts across the construction spectrum. But it didn't happen overnight. It required a lot of hard work. It required effort. It required a lot of the same skills I learned back in grade school all those years ago—trust, faith in myself, humility, humor, and the willingness to take a risk. But I did it, and it made me realize that the path I took wasn't that different from a lot of other successful people without college degrees—people who got their start washing dishes at a restaurant and then rose their way up the line all the way to head chef, or began as an electrical apprentice and ended up owning a fleet of electrical trucks. No matter what you do or hope to achieve, there are no shortcuts. You have to put in the time. You must learn the ropes. You must work hard. But you can do it. You can move up and live the life you want to live— starting today.

Okay, so a quick sidebar story on hard work. I love to use analogies to explain things as it just seems to help create the picture of what I'm trying to convey. Not too long ago, Nancy and I took our daughter, Nicole, to Napa Valley, California, to celebrate her twenty-first birthday. Like most parents, it was hard to imagine our little girl reaching that milestone. Heck, it seems like only yesterday she was eight years old learning to drive a golf cart or fishing old golf balls out of the creek at our club.

Knowing she might not have made it to this milestone made me even more grateful. You see, a little over eight years ago, she was diagnosed with cancer (more on that later) and survived. Her turning twenty-one was nothing short of a miracle, and we wanted to celebrate it in a memorable way. For a few years now, she had heard Nancy and I talk about how beautiful California was, particularly the area of Napa Valley. And so in a fashion that only Nicole could do, she lobbied us with the idea of visiting this amazing place together. We thought, *Why not?* There was no better opportunity to take Nicole to wine country, not because she was now of legal age to drink, and not even that it is one of the most scenic areas in the United States. No, we wanted her to see how wine is made and learn how to smell it, taste it, and even how to swirl the wine in the glass. I don't think you can fully appreciate something until you understand where it comes from—and that goes for both wine and human beings alike!

Now, you're probably asking yourself, *What does wine country have to do with Ken's story and the hard work he has endured to make his dreams a reality?* Well, here's your answer. When Nancy and I first went to Napa Valley many years ago, we learned something we had never known before about making wine. It stuck with me and got me thinking—and it's why the wine industry always makes me think of our brave, courageous Nicole. One of the most interesting parts of the process of turning grapes into great wine lies not above the ground, as you see in the photos of many beautiful wineries. No, the real work, the beginning and most important part of the process, begins way below the surface, where the root takes off.

Most of us have heard about the Napa Valley in sunny California and have seen pictures of its beautiful hills and fertile valleys. We've also heard about its wonderful climate and the dark and rich volcanic soils that are so vital to the growing process.

So it should make perfect sense that some of the great wines in the world are made from the lush purple grapes that grow in this marvelous location, right? Well, no. The truth is, creating a perfect wine grape takes a lot more than sunshine and raindrops. Actually, the opposite conditions may be more relevant to the success of the vines. The irony here is rich. Unlike the first foot or so of that amazing volcanic soil that nourishes a grapevine, the more the vine *struggles* to get through, the harder, rockier, less forgiving, and more uninhabitable the earth, the better-quality grape it produces. In other words, the struggle is what makes the grapes so good. More aptly, the struggle is what makes them *great*. The harder the vine has to work, the better tasting the grape; hence, the better the wine.

That's you—the struggling vine that's going to make great wine. I am going to be real here for a minute. It won't always be easy, and it won't always be pretty, but if you're willing to put in some hard years, you will reap the rewards. To this very day, I still remember being packed into a truck with five guys (who had very different ideas about hygiene) and spending every moment of the day between six thirty a.m. to four p.m. just grinding it out, working my butt off. But I had goals. I had drawn my life. I could see it. I wanted to make money. I wanted to support myself to that end. So I did the work, and a funny thing happened while I did it: I actually ended up enjoying it and getting good at it. I liked the challenge. Most days when I got home, I was sore, tired, dirty, and pissed off. And while there is something about working really hard over a long day that revs you up, you do need time to come down from it. And like I mentioned earlier, when you work with your hands, there is that step-back moment when you take some time to look back at what you just accomplished. And whether I had just saved a broken basement wall, planted a dozen ten-foot pine trees, or created a beautiful stone waterfall for a happy home-owner, I felt a huge sense of satisfaction every day, a huge sense of worth.

I think the appeal is that hard work focuses you. It puts you in the moment. It shows you what you're capable of, and ulti-mately what you can achieve when you challenge your mind and body. It shows you that if you're willing to put yourself in a situation that forces you to work hard and grow, you're putting yourself in a position to achieve comfort, peace, and freedom.

When I was working around the clock in those early years of my working life, I was literally and figuratively digging my-self a solid foundation for the *rest* of my life. It was a rite of pas-sage that only those who have done the same can relate to. A hard day's work gives you a kind of clarity that no other action does. Everyone has to pay their dues. Only you can decide what type of work you're willing to do to get to the next level.

Whether you get your start in a hair salon, bakery, ware-house, restaurant, or waterproofing business, it doesn't matter. There is a path you can take that will lead to a good life. It used to be a familiar and well-worn path, but somehow it was buried (quite possibly by all that student debt I was talking about). All jokes aside, it's a lost path, and I want to reclaim it—for you. I don't want you to be intimidated by the hard work required at the outset. I want to assure you that it's going to be worth it. I also want to assure you that there is a huge demand for people who are willing to learn a trade, provide a service, and join the workforce. Trust me. I've been waiting a year for a stone-mason, who is making a boatload of money, to come to my house to finish a job. *He's* in control. *He* is the supply—basically the only gig in town—and the demand is great, and he is making a fortune because of it!

Again, I want to remind you. He is doing something that most others are NOT. And so that causes a supply-and-demand upheaval. And that, my friends, causes wages to rise. It's a simple principle. Work hard, enjoy the good outdoors, maybe even be your own boss, set your own schedule . . . and make a great living doing it. It's going to take a long time (if ever) before the supply of stonemasons is greater than the demand for them. Law degrees and business majors may be a dime a dozen, but stonemasons and others who know how to operate a saw, tile a floor, or paint a house are not. The need for skilled, able, and willing laborers is not a passing trend. People are going to need workers who know how to *do* things, specifically how to work with their hands, for a long time. Even with the advent of intelligent or mechanized labor, I guarantee that for every baby with a smartphone in his or her hand today, there is going to be a need to hire someone who knows how to use a shovel or a rake or a hammer or a wrench. While today's smartphones can do a lot, they can't do finish carpentry, plumb a house, landscape a yard, run a salon, or have their own retail store or daycare center. Remember that as we move throughout this book.

My story has been a challenging but rewarding one. And I have always believed that each of us is shaped by our own stories of struggle, challenge, and hopefully accomplishment.

I will close this chapter with one of my greatest challenges. A plight that I wouldn't wish on anyone. This story is one of the main drivers of my decision to write this book. And yet it wasn't even me who had to walk this terrible path.

When I think of someone who was made great by enormous

struggle, I need look no further than my incredible daughter, Nicole. Indulge me here, as this will help explain how I arrived at C, P, and F in the first place.

Now, I am fully aware that most parents think their kids are the greatest, and Nancy and I are no exception. A beautiful soul—inside and out—Nicole has endured more serious challenges in her young life than most people three times her age, and yet she has done so with grace, humor, and a positive, can-do attitude. She has not only succeeded, she has flourished and exceeded all our expectations as parents. Most important, she is the kindest person I know. So you'll soon understand why it seems impossible for me to even write these next few words: you see, there was a time not long ago when my wife and I were scared . . . terrified actually . . . that we might lose her, that she might never have the chance to grow up to be the amazing woman she is today.

So here we go, down the path of discovering the three most important words that now rule my life. The good and the bad of 2009. In the first six months of that year, things were good— I mean, really GOOD. Business was booming, and Nancy and I were nearing completion on our dream home, a French country–style design built of antique stone and brick, with beautiful landscaping and gardens. We had been planning this project for several years—a vision we'd been seeing very clearly for a long time. Yes, it was setting up to be a busy summer. I was working hard at the office and golfing whenever I could find the time. Nicole was learning to play softball and golf, playing with her puppies, and just doing what twelve-year-old girls do. Nancy was running her design business and enjoying her gardening at home. We were also getting in plenty of pool time, having barbecues, and running from one social engagement to the next. We were living our best life—or so we thought. Sure, there were obstacles here and there, but things were good, and my daughter was growing up fast, so Nancy and I were enjoying the precious time with her, time that we had worked so hard all these years to create. That was the good.

Now, the BAD. Out of nowhere, our world suddenly came crashing down in one devastating week. Driving to softball practice one evening, Nicole said to us from the back seat, "Something's wrong. I have a shadow in my right eye."

"A shadow? What do you mean, a shadow?" She told us that when she closed her left eye, she could only see out of about half of her right, as if there was a shadow there, running diagonally across it.

Naturally, a million simple explanations ran through my head:

- *Maybe there is dirt in her eye?*
- *Perhaps she scratched it somehow?*
- *Maybe she even has a bit of heatstroke from the ninety-degree day?*

Who knows? I sort of dismissed it. I had experienced a scratched eye in the past, so I knew it would be something that would heal quickly.

However, my wife, God love her, scheduled an appointment with a friend, an optometrist who practiced nearby. He thought it might be a hemangioma, an abnormal buildup of blood vessels in the surface of the eye, which was treatable. He recommended us to an ophthalmologist to confirm his diagnosis.

The next day we went to see the ophthalmologist, who indicated to us that it was a bit more complicated than we had originally thought. He said the buildup in Nicole's eye was putting pressure on the retina, and recommended we see an eye specialist at the Cleveland Clinic.

Now we were nervous, and off we went the next day, driving two hours to see the specialist. There were a bunch of examinations and dozens of digital photographs taken of what the doctors were now calling a "mass." And there was waiting— lots and lots of excruciating waiting. Even though we had a noon appointment, the entire waiting room of other patients were seen and sent on their way before we got our results. In a word, it was torture. Pure torture. All we could do was smile at each other, hope for the best, and hug our precious child.

At 4:20 p.m. that day, after four painful hours, Nancy and I were finally called into the doctor's office. Nicole was asked to remain in the waiting room just outside. This was our first sign that this was not going to be a positive end to an already exhausting process. We didn't know it at the time, but we were just getting started. The nurse who was in the room with the doctor decided to drop a box of tissues in my wife's lap as she left the office. That seemed an odd gesture to me, and as it turned out, it was not a good sign. I clearly remember saying to Nancy, "Did you ask her for those?" She shook her head and turned to me with a now-terrified look on her face. That was the precise moment we knew this was going to be a bad day. And I mean a really bad day.

When the doctor finally greeted us, we could instantly tell he was distraught, avoiding eye contact and having some serious difficulty getting the conversation going. Then the moment came. After a long sigh, the doctor gave us the news. We heard the word fall from his lips as if in slow motion. It was like I could hear every letter: M-E-L-A-N-O-M-A.

We were stunned. I remember grabbing Nancy's hand, which was now shaking. It's a bit of a blur at that point as we asked question after question with little or no relief. How could this happen, when did this happen, how did we miss it? We have no history of this in our family!

The bottom line was that the tumor had to be removed immediately to prevent the cancer from spreading, even if that meant Nicole losing her eye right along with it. The word *devastated* doesn't even begin to cover it.

I spent the next few tearful, sleepless nights poring over everything the internet had to offer about her condition, trying to avoid the scary stuff, focusing instead on what we could do to not only save our little girl, but to make a good life for her as best we could. I found a clinic in Philadelphia that was world-renowned for ocular melanoma treatment and other eye conditions. All those years of working the phones in sales came in handy, and I talked my way past the three-month waiting list to get Nicole an immediate appointment. We left for Philly the next day.

We had been letting Nicole know all along that we were looking at something that was serious and that we were going to get her the best care possible. We told her she was tough, and that we would get through this *as a team*. Throughout the initial diagnosis appointments, the multiple blood tests, and all the poking and prodding, we never heard her complain. But eventually we had to break the grisly news that she had a "bad guy" inside her, we needed to get it out, and the only way to do that was to remove the tumor and, if necessary, her eye.

I remember that day clearly. Every minute of it. Nancy and I privately strained to find the right way to tell her. We struggled until we finally came up with an answer. The three of us often rode our bikes through the neighborhood. This was a peaceful exercise, something we really enjoyed doing, so we thought it would be a good opportunity to break the news. We didn't want to sit her down somewhere and make a big scene of it or scare her. I wanted her to know that the life she enjoyed now was going to be very much the same. We would still be riding bikes—arms spread out wide and free: *Look, Dad, no hands!* I wanted her to know that we were going down this road together, for better or for worse, and that she wasn't alone. So I took her on a slow bike ride and carefully explained that it was time to get rid of the "bad guy." Trying desperately to find the right words, I fumbled a bit. My heart was breaking inside. How was I going to tell my beautiful little girl that we had to remove her eye? It was, without a doubt, the most difficult conversation I have ever had in my life, save for one very bright light—my daughter. It turns out that while I was desperately trying to hold it together—you know, be a strong dad for *her*—it was Nicole who took the proverbial handlebars from me and literally steered us in the right direction. Something amazing happened. She assessed the situation, clearly understood it, and basically said she was ready to do it. And while I will not reveal what she said exactly, I will tell you that she remained tough, vigilant, and more understanding than any twelve-year-old should have been in that situation. She was the strong one. She was not only ready to rid herself of this disease, but also was appreciative for a full life, focusing on what she COULD do versus what she couldn't.

A few weeks later, Nicole underwent an operation to remove the cancer and had a prosthesis attached. After the surgery, she had to undergo several more rounds of testing, and to this day is followed up every six months (and will be for the rest of her life). Anyone who has survived melanoma knows how precarious this disease is. It is called the silent killer for a reason. Most people are unaware that they have it until it is so far advanced that there is nothing anyone can do. And the cancer can break off and appear in distant organs if it's not caught in time. Every time my daughter goes in for a liver ultrasound, Nancy and I experience the torture all over again as we watch the nurse technician click buttons and take pictures that appear before us on a screen. Our minds race, and we are constantly thinking . . . *What are all those marks they are measuring on her liver? What does it mean? Why can't they tell us anything? $%@#, can you just tell me she is okay?* Waiting for the results for days every six months is a level of hell I wouldn't wish on my worst enemy. But Nicole always handles it beautifully and with courage. No one else has ever inspired me more.

Her cancer now gone, she is living a normal life, and we are very thankful for that. Even after all these years, I have never once heard her complain. I see so many girls these days freak out over a hair being out of place, but my Nicole never so much as whined a bit about losing her eye or half her sight. She learned to adapt to her new condition, living a regular life, riding her bike, and doing most of what she could do before. She even became a four-year varsity golfer in high school and was captain of her team. We play together as often as we can, something I look forward to more than anything.

Nicole's dream was to be an architect, so she decided college was right for her. She studied at the University of Miami in Oxford, Ohio, specializing in sustainable, passive house construction and energy-efficient design, and now she is getting her masters at the University of Michigan. She is one of only three certified passive house consultants (a modern-day version of green building) and, as of this writing, the youngest in the country. She quite literally kept her focus on the big picture— her life ahead of her, not dwelling on what she had lost.

So I bet you're wondering what all of this has to do with *comfort, peace, and freedom*? Well, I'll tell you: it has everything to do with it.

I don't like to think about what could have happened if Nancy hadn't had the presence of mind to call the optometrist, or if I hadn't thrown myself into research to find the best doctors in the country. The reality is it would have been a nightmare if we hadn't. Why? Because we would have lost Nicole. Everything we'd worked for—the company, the house, the fun stuff, the lifestyle, everything would have been meaningless without her in our lives. She brings us hope, love, laughter, comfort, peace, and freedom—all of it. And if I had been preoccupied with only making ends meet, if I had been focused on paying the bills, getting to work on time, what my friends thought of me, or any of the other crap that we let occupy our five-gallon-bucket brains, I wouldn't have had the presence of mind to remain calm, cool, and collected and find the help we needed. And Nancy wouldn't have either.

I am sure many of you have already been through quite a lot in your lives, so this may not be a shock to most of you, but I am going to say it anyway: Life is going to throw you some mighty curveballs. You aren't going to see them coming. You aren't going to be prepared. This is part and parcel of life. You are human. You will get sick. Or someone in your family will have an accident. Someone you love will pass away. Not one of us gets off this planet without loving and losing. Natural disasters strike. Economic slumps happen every decade or so. There are going to be as many highs as there are lows in life. You can't be 100 percent prepared for all of them. I know friends whose lives have been turned upside down by murder, drugs, natural disasters, health scares, and financial difficulties. No one gets through life without facing at least one struggle, if not many. Like the craggy dirt the grapevines must contend with, these struggles are what make us better. They toughen us up, and I hope they also make us more compassionate and grateful people who can savor the moments that are good, even when things seem impossible.

Going through an experience like what we did with Nicole changes you, plain and simple. Suddenly, all those daily aggravations and frustrations we encounter just don't seem to register with the power they once had. They become what some like to refer to as "small ball," meaning they reside in the minor, minor leagues, never to reach the majors. You begin to look at life in a new and different way. Your perspective is permanently altered, and you begin to feel like you need to share this new feeling with others to help them avoid wasting years of their lives in trial and error, eventually learning things by experience. It is with this very fact in mind that I began to write a letter to Nicole. The purpose of this letter was to try to get her to see, very early in her life, that while she was going through some serious struggles, there are indeed some important things we all should really focus on, visualize, and aspire to. In other words, things that REALLY matter. And lo and behold, after twelve full legal pads, many ink pens, and the occasional sore wrist, that long letter became the start of this significantly lengthier book!

3

COMFORT, PEACE, AND FREEDOM

I have been thinking about the real meaning of life for a very long time. As you get on in life and you experience more and more of what this world has to offer, you begin to value and prioritize certain things over others, and that tends to present to you a whole new perspective of what is truly meaningful. What is truly important. This can happen at any age, and I contend, the earlier the better.

Now, I have been asked many times about the origin of these three words, and about how they came to be so important in my life. I believe C, P, and F (comfort, peace, and freedom, of course) are inexorably connected to one another, just like a triangle, with each one having the same amount of weight and influence. And each one makes the others stronger. Remove any one of them, and the triangle falls apart. That is what gives these three words their strength.

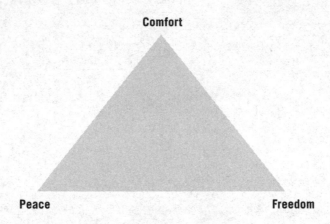

Now, you could say that one of these concepts obviously leads to the others (comfort, then peace, then freedom), and you would be correct. It's just that in my opinion, as they come to fruition in your life, they constantly bounce off one another in a stream of support, just as they do in a triangle. However, if you choose to believe that one leads to the others in a more linear fashion, then it will be important to realize that once you have arrived at freedom, the cycle begins to build on itself much like a hurricane. Taken literally, freedom can just as easily work in reverse to create more comfort, which can support even more peace in your day, and so on.

The good news is you can see it either way, as both get you to the same great place.

COMFORT

Let's talk about the first point in the triangle, *comfort*. I'm willing to wager that my definition of the word *comfort* is probably a bit different from what you think it means. So just for fun, let's define this word as I found it in different dictionaries, just so we have a base meaning. Here we go:

- **Comfort**—*a state or situation where you are relaxed, the feeling of being less worried, to be able to afford or enjoy contentment.*

Most of us have ideas or pictures that come to mind as soon as we think of the word *comfort*. However, the way I will be talking about it does not necessarily relate to the type of clothes you like to wear, or what type of furniture you like to lounge on, or even what type of home you envision yourself living in. Early on, we discussed the idea of drawing what you want your life to look like and how you see it unfolding for you. Nothing has changed there. You still need to create shelter for yourself, and that certainly comes in many different forms. And if you are going to go through this process, you should land on that which ultimately makes you comfortable. I am giving you total artistic license here. If you want an apartment in the city with a huge comfy sectional, a beanbag chair, a swing in the corner, and a seventy-five-inch TV on the wall . . . go for it. Those are typically called "creature comforts," and we all want them to be just how we see them in our mind's eye.

But I'd like to add to that concept a bit. I want to explore the idea of comfort as it refers to the path that leads to an overall life of *comfort*, *peace*, and *freedom*. The comfort I am now describing is foundational, meaning it is within YOU. It is *you* who needs to feel a sense of comfort about who you can be.

Have you ever heard someone describe someone else as a person who is "comfortable in her own skin"? Do you know what that phrase really means? I think I do. It means that she is comfortable with who she is. Ask yourself if you are comfortable with *who you are.* Are you comfortable with the direction your life is heading? Are you comfortable with what you do for a living? The way you choose to spend your time? How you are perceived by others? And finally, are you comfortable with sharing your talents and skills to benefit others?

Ironically, in today's world of job opportunities, achieving a life of comfort can mean going outside one's "comfort zone" to choose what is now largely considered an unconventional road—taking a risk to plow one's own path. Ultimately, it means choosing a career and a path that will provide you what you need, while living your best life, one that is free of unnecessary financial or work stress—in other words, one that will create comfort for you, in all of its forms. Your definition of *comfort* could mean that you are not chasing labels, struggling to keep up with the Joneses, or doing what you hate just to pay the bills. Rather, *comfort* means doing what you love and being in control of your life and your choices—and being *comfortable* with them. It means being able to get up each day and say, "I am in control of what I want, what I envision, what I anticipate, and what I can do for a living that will take me there . . . and I like what I see!" The bottom line here is that being comfortable with yourself and your decisions and who you are and what you stand for means being open to life in the present moment and open to all sorts of possibilities and opportunities.

Last word on comfort. I think we all should be keenly aware of our own strengths and weaknesses. Being able to accept that academics is something you're not good at, or maybe you don't care all that much about, is an important part of self-awareness, and ultimately your ability to stay present. If you're not happy with how your world is progressing, or not very comfortable with your career decisions or your own abilities and limitations, you'll likely wind up sitting at your desk wishing for a different life. What I want to do for you is to help you broaden your outlook on what you can do for a living to support your life drawing.

Remember again the stonemason who worked on my home? Now here's a man who is comfortable with who he is, what he's good at, and knows exactly how he wants to spend his days. He would roll up to a house each morning in his brand-new bright red Ford pickup with his crew right behind him. He would jump out of that truck, wearing his "uniform" of jeans, a T-shirt, work boots, a smile on his face, and a cup of coffee in hand. He'd arrive ready to take on the day . . . his day, the way he wanted it. Funny, I never got the feeling these guys wanted to be anywhere else than with one another . . . working away, listening to Led Zeppelin, singing and laughing with one another while they artfully crafted (with their bare hands) the most beautiful fences and patios out of huge piles of stone. The talented stonemason and his crew were satisfied, happy, content, in control, and most of all, comfortable. They were blue-collar cool—working hard, making a great living, runnin' their own show. Simply doing what they love to do. Something I believe we should all aspire to.

PEACE

Okay, so now it's peace's turn. Just as with comfort, I think it best to start off this section on peace with a definition, again culled from the best dictionaries available, which will give us a base meaning from which we can build upon.

- **Peace:** *in a general sense, a state of quiet or tranquility, freedom from disturbance, to temper the mind.*

When I think of peace, I think of setting myself up to experience a peaceful existence, and doing so *far in advance*, in a way that most people never envision, much less achieve. But don't worry, when I use the word *peace*, I am not doing it to get all hippie or spiritual on you. Nor am I intending to share the oft-recommended Zen approach to life. I will say, though, you may find my approach to living a life of comfort, peace, and freedom to be a kind of working person's Zen, or blue-collar coolness, if you will. I can assure you you're not going to be required to sit in a lotus position, meditate, or burn incense to achieve the level of peace I'm talking about. No, you'll see the kind of peace we're after is attained by a *choice*. Once you make it, peace will flow naturally within you and throughout all of your days. What is that choice? It is the decision to put your life in play, to put yourself first and take the necessary actions required to both set and follow the personal and career goals *you* have set for *yourself*, which will ultimately provide you with the life you have envisioned. You most certainly will attain peace by being present—fully present. And by that, I mean being engaged with the task at hand. Peace is the opposite of being stressed and anxious. Being present means not looking to the past with anger or resentment, and it means not being fearful of the future. Being present means you have the here and now, and you take life one step at a time, one day at a time. If you do this, before you know it, that future you were once so worried about will be right there in front of you, and you will be able to look back on all your wonderful achievements.

In a previous chapter, we talked about looking into the future and envisioning your life six months, one year, three years, and even five to ten years down the road. Peace comes from putting the plan into actual practice. I'm going to date myself here, but as a kid we used to have a football board game comprised of small plastic players that we would position on a metal football field. You and your opponent would line up your team, eleven on each side, in football formation. One side was the offense, the other defense. Once both teams were set, you would flip a switch and the plastic football field would begin to vibrate. The players would begin to move, hopefully in the direction you wanted them to go, with your blockers leading your running back down the field, or if you were on defense, your linemen cutting through to make the tackle—all from the random way the vibrations would propel your little plastic men around the field.

I can hear some of you saying, "Hey, I remember that game!" It's a game from the seventies called Electric Football. Believe it or not, you can still find vintage versions of the game for sale on the internet. You can also see demonstrations on YouTube of players carefully planning their next plays, taking great care to line their team up just right before hitting the electric switch so the play will, hopefully, unfold exactly as envisioned.

When I think of the game design of Electric Football, the word *anticipation* comes to mind. The plan is set, the go button is hit, and the anticipation of a result is on.

Anticipation goes hand in hand with the idea of peace. "What?!" you say. But think about it. Anticipation is the path that leads to peace. In the coming chapters, you will hear me discuss in great detail how to live a life of anticipation, and how doing so will create a sense of peace within you. In my opinion, there is no other way to live.

Anticipation is the excitement of waiting eagerly for something you know is going to occur. An excited expectation of an event. Preparing to take an action based on a previous plan. So how exactly do we take that concept and apply it to ourselves and our own situations? I guarantee that doing so will improve how you live your life.

You might ask, what kind of things can we plan and then eagerly anticipate? Well, there are many. You can schedule dinner with friends, a party, or a birthday celebration. You can go further with more consequential plans, like a Christmas savings account, a retirement plan, vacations, home-buying strategies— the more the better. You may notice I have listed short-term goals that are possible to meet within days or weeks, as well as longer-term goals that may take months or years. Why? Because you should endeavor to preplan as much of your life as possible. It will allow you to swim around in a pool of constant anticipation, eagerly and anxiously and happily waiting on the event, result, or accomplishment to appear. And why do all of this? It's quite simple, actually. You do it because it gives you peace.

Here's a pretty common example of what I am talking about—something that most of us do already. Let's say you plan a vacation for next year. You get busy with all the details, set the dates, book a hotel room, plan your route, maybe reserve a plane ticket, and most important, start saving money. And then what? You sit back, relax, and wait for it to happen. You anticipate the day with excitement. "We're going to the lake this summer. I can hardly wait!" is often heard. It brings you peace to know that you have it all handled.

What if the rest of your life was that way? Remember, life has a way of throwing unexpected things at you, some pleasant and some not so. And you will want to be present for that and roll with those events. But just think of the level of peace it could bring you. I'm here to tell you it can be all of that and more. Peaceful. It *should* be. It *will* be. And I will show you how.

As you can tell, my take on the word *peace* is designed to inspire positive, motivating feelings to those fortunate enough to experience it. As I said early on, this is not a calm, prayer-like type of peace. Rather, it is an energy-filled state of mind excited by the future. And what makes it even better is that it is a conscious decision. You can decide right now, this very day, if you want to have this form of peace in your life. The choice is yours. Could this kind of peace be within you? I think so.

FREEDOM

By now, I think you get the drill, so in the spirit of being consistent, let's begin this final section on *freedom* by once again providing the meaning of the word culled from the major dictionaries:

- **Freedom:** *the state of being free, the absence of constraint in choice or action, not having necessity or coercion, the opportunity to pursue one's happiness.*

Just as we have shown with the first two concepts, comfort and peace, the word *freedom* can have different meanings to different people, so I will give you my thoughts on the concept of being free. I mean truly free. Free in your mind. Free in your outlook on life. Maybe creating some free space in that busy head of yours. Free to choose how you want to spend your time and your money. And finally, free to choose how you live.

If you were to look back on what we have learned thus far about comfort and peace, you would almost certainly draw some simple conclusions that relate to the idea of **freedom**. One would be that we are **free** to define what it is that makes us feel comfortable. You and only you can do that. Just like the life drawing we made early on in this book, we can put down on paper the things we want to surround ourselves with, and once that is accomplished, we have that much less to think about. Let's go back to planning a major event. Once all the choices are made and we have that task completed, we have less to occupy our minds with. All the stresses, anxieties, necessities, and coercions are behind us. This is entirely **freeing**.

The same holds true for the peace that comes from living a well-planned life, full of anticipation as you eagerly await the next opportunity, milestone, or phase. Remember the fifth gallon in our five-gallon-bucket head—the place where all our emotions, good or bad, fight for valuable space in which to hang out? Well, I submit that the feeling of freedom is an emotion . . . a very powerful, positive one. Imagine having so little negative energy in your head that you allow spontaneity to live and breathe. Or how about having so much space up there that love, affection, creativity, and charity can all move right in and stay as long as they want? How would your daily decisions change if you had those guests staying upstairs, instead of the . . . let's say, the Addams family? You know who I'm talking about—fear, anger, frustration, jealousy, depression. You recognize them, don't you?

The reality is that just like good feelings beget good feelings, freedom begets freedom. When you start making deliberate choices for yourself and how you use your time, before you know it you are doing things that make you feel freer, more self-reliant, and more *alive*. Your ultimate path to freedom requires that you acknowledge the preciousness of your time. After taking stock of what you're doing, you can then start focusing on what you want. There is an incredible freedom in living a life you're in charge of, doing things that make you feel comfortable, peaceful, and free. You already have everything you need inside of you. And you also have time. As short as our time is on earth, the amount of time in a day is the same for everyone on the planet. We're all operating with the same twenty-four hours. And *you* get to decide what *you* do with that time. You get to decide what desired feelings and experiences you want to have. You get to choose your ultimate path to freedom. You can do whatever it is you want to do with your "free time" once you put your goal paths into action.

I will close this chapter with a story. I promised you early on that in this book I would share with you my experiences in the blue-collar world and how they built who I am today. I promised to help you think better, to visualize better, to plan better, and to open your mind to opportunities so that you can take advantage of the blue-collar supply-and-demand volatility. I said I would help you set goals that you can actually hit, and I will soon show you how to do that and make your plans bulletproof. I also promised to share some stories of others I have met along the way who embody this plan for life and who have taught me a thing or two (whether they knew it at the time or not). This is one of those stories. It is the epitome of C, P, and F, and it is rooted in **simplicity**. Life lived in a very simple way.

Let's begin, as we always do when discussing these important words, by offering up a definition, in this case of the word
simplicity:

- The quality or condition of being plain or natural.
- A thing that is plain, natural, or easy to understand.

Many years ago, I was fortunate enough to meet someone who embodies a life well lived—a deviously **simple**, well-
planned life to be sure. And while his vision for living may not
be for everyone, I am certain that *nearly* everyone can and will
appreciate it. He is a blue-collar hero of mine. I call him the
"Grass Cutter from Minnesota," or just "Minnesota" for short. I
call him that because I never caught his name, even though we
once spent a week with this guy many years ago.

In January of that year, several of my coworkers and I decided to escape the cold, gray, snowy northern Ohio winter and
head to Cancún for some much-needed respite and sunshine.
At the end of each day in the sun, most of us headed to the
main bar, full of fun-seekers from all over the world. Naturally,
it didn't take long for a bunch of ditch diggers from Ohio to
discover another Midwesterner looking to drink some tequila,
which our group did . . . a lot. Turns out, he was kind of like
us, a hardworking guy in his late twenties just trying to escape
the cold. Over the next few days, we would run into him at
the bar and invariably spend a lot of time swapping stories of
quirky customers, strange employees, you name it. However,
soon we would figure out that Minnesota wasn't *entirely* like us.
It was quite obvious he was a lot tanner than anyone else at the
resort, and coming from the Upper Midwest, which in January
can be almost akin to Alaska, this seemed highly unlikely. But

it was more than that. His demeanor had an eerie calm to it. I guess you could say he had a tranquility about him, an intense peace . . . much more so than the rest of us temporary visitors. And we noticed that nearly all of the resort workers knew him well. Hmm, something was afoot.

It was then that I spotted several different neon-colored Club Med bracelets on Minnesota's wrist. Seven in all, which was six more than any of the rest of us had. And then the pieces started to come together.

Turns out that at most all-inclusive resorts like Club Med, the bracelet you're given signifies weekly membership. The bracelets change colors each week so that Club Med employees can differentiate quickly between the comers and the goers. Pretty **simple** concept, eh? Well, Minnesota had *seven* of these bands on his wrist, and we soon figured out why everyone seemed to know him so well. "Dude, what's with all the wristbands?" I asked. Well, Minnesota just sat back in his chair, big smile on his face, and shot his tequila. He then went on to explain the reason for all those wristbands. You see, he spent a week at eight different Club Meds each year! I couldn't believe what I was hearing. *My group has busted their backs all year just to be able to afford one week*, I thought. Minnesota went on to say that he carefully planned his life to allow him to make this possible, and in doing so, he also committed himself to a **simplified** life. During the spring, summer, and fall, he ran his small landscape company—mowing lawns, trimming and edging beds, spreading mulch, and raking leaves. He had a few employees, and they all worked really hard from sunup to sundown for ten straight months. In doing that, he told us, he earned enough money to pay his employees, cover his bills, and save enough to afford his escape from the harsh Upper Midwest winters at a

Club Med tropical paradise in locations all across the Caribbean and the world. He later shared with us that he keeps his home life relatively simple so he can be away so long.

We began to appreciate the mind-set of the Grass Cutter from Minnesota. Because he knew that travel and escaping the winter was a priority for him, he didn't bog himself down with a giant mortgage, credit cards, or large car payments. He had a clear picture of what his comfort, peace, and freedom looked like. Satisfied with a small house and a five-year-old pickup truck, he was able to live the life he wanted. He didn't have much debt, and he shared with me how he divvied up his own paycheck each week to save all year long for his precious and well-earned time off. Since he stayed at the resorts so long, he was also able to negotiate a discount that gave him a much more affordable eight-week rate. Genius, no? Just think of it for a moment: he had fifty-six straight days of feet in the sand, windsurfing, kayaking, paddleboarding, hiking, fishing, meeting an ever-changing group of interesting people, downing tropical drinks, and eating great food, not to mention being waited on hand and foot. He could do whatever he felt like, when he felt like it, for an unbelievable eight weeks every winter. And with his very blue-collar career, he took control of his own destiny and planned out his happy time well in advance, down to every specific detail. He exemplified the practice of living his life in anticipation, and of **simplicity**, and with that came enormous peace.

Most people might say, "That's impossible." But it's not. Minnesota designed the life exactly like he wanted it, and by living **simply** he was able to live better than most millionaires. It's an amazing feat, and yet so amazingly **simple**. Because he was able to live **simply** and prioritize what mattered to him, he could create a life that afforded him not only comfort (and I am talking Club Med–level comfort), but more important, peace and freedom. Yes, the Grass Cutter from Minnesota loved the life he envisioned, the life he had planned, the life he lived.

I said at the outset that the way Minnesota spent his days may not be for everybody, and that is certainly true. But if you are truly interested in making the best version of you that you can, then you need to ask yourself these questions:

- *Am I capable of seeing my life exactly how Minnesota does?*
- *Do I have the ability to put that into action?*
- *What might be MY Club Med paradise?*

This is very important because as you will see throughout this book, we will discuss the opportunities that the blue-collar world has to offer you. And if you can pair that up with a clear vision of who you are and who you want to be? The world will be your Club Med.

4

AMERICA—LAND OF THE FREE, HOME OF THE SKILLED

Have you ever wondered where the term *blue collar* came from? Well, *I* have, and it turns out that this word has more than one origin story, so I will share with you the explanation that most resonates with me.

The story goes that in the early 1900s, workers and day laborers weren't required to wear a particular color shirt to work, unlike office workers, who were required to wear a shirt with a white collar. Laborers needed to wear comfortable clothing, and as it turns out, most dungaree-type casual work shirts came in the color blue. These shirts were easy to care for, and people could work in them without fear of soiling the crisp white collar worn by their office counterparts.

Interesting, no? And so, while we were researching the material for this book, we came across some interesting facts and trends on the origins of the blue-collar workers themselves. Who were these early blue-collar workers? Where did they come from? What skills, personality traits, and characteristics did they bring to our country? Now, something else must be said here. We have heard so many times about how our country was built from the sweat and hard work of our ancestors, nearly all of whom immigrated here from other countries. We've heard how they took a chance, left their families, and came to America to seek a better life.

Came to America. Have you ever thought what *that* means, exactly? To answer that question is to fully understand how to be successful in today's blue-collar world. What do I mean? It's simply this. If you take a closer look at what it took to be an immigrant who "came to America" to begin anew, you will clearly see how you too can build your life exactly how you see it. I'll explain.

Let's examine the plight of the typical European immigrant. Here you have an able-bodied human being, motivated by who knows what, who packs all their belongings into a small sack, scrapes together enough money to buy a one-way ticket on a large transport ship, says goodbye to his or her entire family, and embarks on a monthlong, grueling journey across the ocean. Upon arrival, they literally have no idea where their next meal will come from, much less where they might sleep that very evening. They arrive with nothing more than a vivid dream of a better life, and a work ethic to match.

Put yourself in that position for a moment. Live that month on the transport ship in your head. Imagine the challenges they had to endure. Just imagine the **faith** it must have taken to make that decision and take that journey with the hope and prayer that they would travel safely. Just imagine the **courage** they had, to arrive in a strange new world with no idea where it would lead them. These are but two of the characteristics that define successful people. Let's take a look at who they were and how they found their way to our great land.

For those who arrived in America in the late nineteenth and early twentieth century, mostly from Europe, the road from laborer to entrepreneur was more difficult than it is today. But still not impossible. Most immigrants during this period arrived from rural communities across the sea, but once in America they were most likely to settle in large cities, like New York and Chicago. As the Industrial Revolution was underway, they went to work in factories, creating a new industrial working class in America. The typical worker began their day in a factory in the early morning and returned after dark. They may have dreamed about joining the middle class, but they were pleased enough to have steady jobs and sufficient income to support their families.

And they sure worked hard. Their unifying factor was that they came to America for a better life and were willing to do anything necessary to achieve it. They were accustomed to struggle. If they had to walk three miles, even if it was carrying buckets (or digging ditches), they would do it. They had a work ethic that was unparalleled because their life had been tough in the country of their birth. They developed a trade because they were easily adaptable to something new and difficult. It didn't seem difficult to them. If you asked them to do something that was tough, they would say, "Count me in." They and their sons and daughters worked hard, and opportunity soon knocked. As these newcomers became accustomed to America, and as second and third generations became fully acclimated, they began different businesses to supplement their family's income.

Sometimes they took in laundry, sold homemade baked goods, or set out a shingle as a "handyman."

Many of these mom-and-pop shops grew into large businesses. Examples can be found everywhere. Legendary Mc-Donald's CEO Ray Kroc was born to parents from Eastern Europe and dropped out of high school. Later in life, he helped build the giant fast-food chain. Likewise, billionaire investor Kerkor Kerkorian was born to immigrant parents from Armenia. He dropped out of school in the eighth grade.

Some nineteenth-century immigrants, of course, arrived in America already skilled. For example, thousands of Eastern European coal miners emigrated to the anthracite and bituminous mines of Pennsylvania. Many became mine managers and executives. German immigrants took jobs as skilled laborers, including jewelry makers, musical instrument manufacturers, cabinetmakers, and tailors. They also worked in groceries, bakeries, and restaurants. One famous German immigrant from Akron, Ohio, near where I live, was Ferdinand Schumacher, who opened a mill there and, with hard work, grew it into a successful business. He is most famous, though, for creating oat squares and flakes that soldiers and civilians alike could easily consume during the Civil War. You might recognize that company today as the Quaker Oats Company. In fact, you've probably eaten his oatmeal. This is a company that exists to this day, based solely on one man's oatmeal recipe, a belief in himself, and a whole lotta hard work.

America was built on the sweat and hard work of these people—the likes of blacksmiths, masons, seamstresses, welders, and carpenters. Most people who immigrated to the United States did so voluntarily. Even those who came here because severe economic hardships caused them to make the painful decision to leave family and friends, made that fateful choice of their own free will. While at the time they may have thought they possessed no other viable options, no one forced them to take the risk, that perilous journey.

Unfortunately, this wasn't the case for everyone. No honest discussion of who helped build America can possibly omit the millions of people who came here involuntarily. We would be remiss if we did not discuss those workers who gave enormous effort to help shape what is now the economic engine that is America.

The exact dates of the origins of slavery in America are a bit unclear, but some historians point to an important period around the very early 1600s, when a ship docked in the English colony of Virginia carrying more than twenty enslaved Africans, who were immediately sold to the colonists. Not yet America, this new world's agricultural boom was in its infancy, but according to the colonial-era *Virginia Gazette*, while most enslaved African Americans worked as farm laborers, they also performed nearly eighty other occupations. They were bricklayers, butchers, cabinetmakers, carpenters, dressmakers, drivers, firemen, fishermen, millwrights, miners, seamstresses, and stonemasons. In short, African Americans are an important part of our history. They should be remembered for their suffering and acknowledged for the major contributions they made to the foundation of our economy, which lasts to this very day.

That's the legacy of many of our ancestors. Today, it's never been easier to break out of the limitations of where you were born and the expectations of others and to use your unique talents to build your own life. With hard work, and with the lessons laid out in the upcoming chapters, I promise you that you can achieve your American dream, however you define it.

And two points about that. One, I'm talking about your own particular definition of the American dream, of a successful life. And two, it doesn't necessarily require a college degree.

FAITH—A BELIEF IN SOMETHING, A SINCERE TRUST, A SYSTEM OF RELIGION

Let's talk about another of the important characteristics that exist in people who have stepped out of their comfort zone and succeeded in life on their own terms. It's having *faith*. Actually, I think *faith* is where it all starts.

When I use the word *faith*, I'm not referring to it in the context of a specific religion. For me, *faith* means believing in something bigger than yourself. It means accepting that you are not fully in control of all life's circumstances, so it means letting go and allowing grace to work through you. Not everyone in life is on the same path, and not everyone is at the same place in their journey. Some people's paths in life are incredibly difficult. Being faithful requires that you have hope that a better day will come. Being faithful means accepting your mistakes and limitations and knowing others have them too, and finding it in your heart to be compassionate—to help others when they are in need. It means that no one is beyond being saved, and that second chances are possible.

When I think of the word *faith* and what it means to have this character trait, I immediately think of Jim Moline. I met Jim in 1987, when I was first starting my own business. Jim, a local builder, helped me navigate the complicated building permit process. Our paths didn't cross again for the next decade, during which time he came to be known in construction circles as an honest, hardworking builder with a great reputation. Though he is the owner of his company, to this day he is often seen working side by side with his framing crews when they get behind schedule. No matter how successful he becomes, he's never felt too important to get his hands dirty. Yes, Jim Moline is the type of guy who is happy to swing a hammer and do whatever it takes to help build the home of someone's dreams. As a result, when my wife, Nancy, and I set out to choose a builder for the home *we* were planning, we interviewed several firms and ultimately selected Jim's.

Over the next several months of construction, Jim and I got to know each other well. We learned a lot about each other's pasts, including how we grew up and came to be involved in what we now did for a living. It was during one of those end-of-day discussions that I learned about Jim's challenging childhood and his extraordinary path to becoming an accomplished builder.

Jim's childhood was, in a word, *harrowing*. By the time he turned two, his parents had divorced, and his mother soon married an abusive alcoholic. Throughout most of his childhood, Jim was beaten and berated, if not by his mother, then by his alcoholic stepfather. He had no comfort, no security, and little love. If not for his grandparents, he would have had no one in his life whom he could trust and emulate.

When Jim was sixteen, his mom threw him out of the house, and he was forced to live with his biological father, with whom he had had very little contact. It was clear to Jim that his father didn't want to have much to do with him.

Like so many others facing heartache, abandonment, and psychological pain, Jim found comfort in the dark forces of drugs and alcohol. He spent many of his teenage days getting high to temporarily escape his chaotic world. He supported his habit by selling pot to his friends at school.

During one Christmas break, Jim met some of these so-called friends to get high. When he arrived, he found they were preparing to shoot heroin. Nervously, as this was a place Jim had not previously gone, he decided to just smoke a bit of heroin instead. Within hours, and after some serious chiding, Jim was injecting it into a vein in his arm. That was it. He was hooked. He would spend the next few weeks making friends with a tiny silver spoon, a lighter, a rubber strap, and a twenty-two-gauge hypodermic needle.

At just seventeen, Jim was now a full-blown drug addict. The next several years played out as you might expect. He spiraled deeper and deeper into his addiction, numbing his pain. Apart from an auto shop teacher who made attempts (to no avail) to intervene, no one took any notice or tried to help him.

Not long after high school graduation, Jim was arrested for a DUI and possession and intent to distribute narcotics. It would be just the first of many more rock bottoms and arrests. He nearly killed himself not once, but twice—first from an overdose from which he was lucky to survive, and then from a car crash while he was high. He would get sober for a while, start working, and then the old demons would rear their ugly heads and he would again succumb to his addictions. Each time when he thought he would be sent to prison, someone—a judge, his grandfather, stepmom, or a probation officer—would intervene on his behalf and give him a second chance—or more like a second, third, and fourth chance. One probation officer, Sergeant

Cynthia Willard, who was tough as nails, recommended a sentence of a year and a half in a supervised halfway house. She watched over him and demonstrated that she believed in him—that she had *faith* in him. She saw something in him that most others couldn't or didn't want to see—most important, what he couldn't see in himself. He would remember and cherish her belief in him for the rest of his life.

At twenty-three years old, Jim decided to commit his life to his own **faith**. He began working every day on his sobriety and making amends with the people he had harmed while on drugs. He spent the next two years working with his stepfather, who had also become sober and was making amends just as Jim was.

Jim was now partial to giving people second chances, as *he* had been given, and he set out alongside his stepfather to learn the ins and outs of carpentry. These were good times, as he rebuilt the relationship that had been ruined years earlier. He came to admire the sober version of his stepfather and was appreciative of the opportunity he was giving him. With the experience he gained, he soon found work with a local builder and continued to hone his skills as a framing carpenter, running crews, and building homes.

But Jim also knew he wanted to pursue his own path, to chart his own course and create the life for himself that he wanted. If he could only catch a well-deserved break. But for the moment, it was just the opposite. Work slowed at his job, and once again he found himself alone and unemployed. He remembers pulling into a parking lot, putting his head in his hands, and sobbing, praying that someone would help him find his path. Someone must have been listening, and when an opportunity presented itself, he jumped for it.

A few weeks passed, and Jim found himself in a local gym where he worked out occasionally. While waiting to use a machine, he struck up a conversation with a gentleman he had seen at a recent church retreat. When he heard that Jim was a framing carpenter, his eyes lit up. "I'm just getting ready to break ground on a spec home. Would you like to frame it?"

Of course, Jim immediately said yes. He assembled a crew and started his own framing business, all because of this one chance meeting. And the work kept coming. For the next five years, Jim stayed busy, learning all he could about running a framing crew. By the time he was thirty, he had built his first home, and two years later, in 1991, Moline Builders, a full-service construction company, was born. Jim proudly remembers winning a bid over a veteran builder on a new condominium within a golf course development. After that project was completed and became a success, the good word spread, and Moline Builders would go on to build two hundred more projects. All in all, his company has seen enormous growth, constructing over five hundred custom homes and condominiums over the past thirty years. Jim has also won the Greater Toledo Choice Awards' Builder of the Year award seven times. He has expanded to include both a building and a development company, both of which continue to thrive today.

I see Jim often these days, driving his perfectly kept pickup truck around town. He still has that laid-back jeans-and-work-boots style that has worked so well for him over the years. He is thriving and building a great life for himself in a blue-collar world. While he is as busy as ever, he is never too busy to give back. He is heavily involved in volunteer work for Habitat for Humanity, helping to build a local church, and volunteering at local shelters and charities around the city. He and his wife, Leann, have three children and a grandchild.

To me, Jim's story is the story of *faith*—faith in God perhaps, but just as important, faith in the human spirit, faith in oneself. So many times people stepped in and gave Jim another chance, despite his repeated failures. So many times Jim accepted those second chances. So many times he had to forgive those who had harmed him, and ask other people for *their* forgiveness.

Jim Moline is like so many young people who I've worked with over the years. They come from tough upbringings; often they haven't received the breaks life offered others. They had to struggle to find peace and comfort within themselves. In some cases, they've also had to turn their lives over to their **faith**. Jim enthusiastically turned his life over to his church. Though he had many relapses in his youth before committing his life to his **faith**, he ultimately overcame his addictions with the help of a lot of prayer, second chances, and people who believed in him. He also began to believe in what others—Mr. Kirby, his auto shop teacher; Cynthia, his probation officer; and his reformed stepfather—saw in him: that he was a person worth saving. That we all are.

I hope Jim's story impacts you as much as it did me. I hope if you're reading this and feeling a bit hopeless, or if you think you're a lost cause and never going to be able to overcome whatever pain or heartbreak you're enduring, you can see that there is redemption for all of us. Jim uses his gifts and talents as a carpenter to give back, to spend his days helping and serving others. In fact, in an amazing twist of fate, one day he was even able to build Cynthia, who was probably the most important stranger to first believe in him, a home of her own.

My wish is that, no matter how low you feel, no matter how hopeless your life and prospects seem today, you can rewrite your destiny. And I know that with **faith** in yourself, you can achieve anything. However, for those times when you do feel a bit down, I hope you can think of Jim Moline and the life he quite literally built for himself and his family.

One last word on **faith**. As you can see, this concept has many meanings based on the given context. As we discussed earlier, for example, the Welsh families who came to America from Scotland, Ireland, and Wales in the mid-1800s? It first took an enormous amount of raw **faith** to travel halfway across the world to establish a new life. **Faith** in themselves and in their god. And they became farmers and builders and ironworkers throughout the Midwest. And they believed, worked hard, and stayed the course to become successful business owners who built coal cars, slate roofs, marble columns, and furniture companies. And all the while they celebrated and relied upon their **faith** in states like Minnesota, where they built nearly forty churches and small chapels. They were driven, and they worked hard, because they believed.

COURAGE—FIRMNESS OF MIND IN THE FACE OF DIFFICULTIES

Like I said, I'm going to be telling you about the most important characteristics that make up the self-made, successful person. Resilience, persistence, generosity, freedom, and commitment will all come in later chapters. But now, after exploring the importance of faith, let's talk about *courage*, another character trait I consider imperative to achieving your life goals.

We throw around the word *courage* a lot these days. In some cases, using the word is warranted, as in the feats of the Olympic athlete, or the soldier on the battlefield. It takes some serious **courage** to ski down a hill at eighty miles per hour, grab a football and run headfirst into a wall of angry men, be a single parent raising kids, or travel to a foreign land to defend our freedoms. There are many forms of courage, and I applaud all those who personify it on a daily basis.

Let's take this a bit deeper. When I use the word *courage*, it means doing something another person would not be willing to do. It doesn't mean being fearless. Rather, it means being afraid of something—but doing the scary, fearsome thing anyway. It means stepping out of your comfort zone and going down a path few others are willing to walk. It means that even when things seem impossibly difficult, you don't yield, you don't give up. In most cases, the biggest rewards (success, satisfaction, even money) are found in places where fewer and fewer of us are willing to go.

For most of my life, I have had a front-row seat to witness this behavior, this characteristic we call **courage**. That's because when I think of **courage**, I think of none other than my own father, Stan Rusniaczyk.

I suppose my dad's upbringing had a lot to do with why I equate **courage** with him. He was courageous at an early age, having done more by the age of twelve than many grown adults have. Born on August 13, 1938, the only child to Walter and Rose, he grew up on the east side of Cleveland in a house so small most would consider it a garage. His father had bought it for $1,800. My dad remembers it being so small that the front yard, if you could call it that, was just three by eight. Yep, three feet by eight feet, with no grass, in a tough, predominantly

Polish, working man's neighborhood. Yet despite the simple conditions, by all accounts my dad had a relatively normal upbringing. He spent nearly eighteen years in that two-bedroom, one-bath bungalow with his parents, learning about life and how to find his way.

In those years, a young boy quickly became a man, and that was no different for Dad. And so, at just twelve years of age, he landed his very first job. When you first hear of a boy that young getting a job, something relatively common, easy, and safe comes to mind, like a newspaper route, or perhaps shoveling driveways in the winter. Stan's first job was different. It required him to take a train and then a bus to downtown Cleveland to work at a printing press, Cromwell Crooks Incorporated. Can you imagine today a young boy at twelve, getting on not one but two forms of public transportation and heading off to, of all things, *his job*? Talk about **courage**.

He would spend nearly two years making that daily journey downtown. His job was to deliver newly printed paperwork all over the city—sometimes walking through traffic, taking another bus, even hailing cabs to make his deliveries. And he did it with firmness of mind in the face of difficulty.

At some point, Dad decided he would move on to his next endeavor. It seemed he discovered that washing cars was a more lucrative occupation, and so off he went, bleaching whitewalls, scrubbing wire wheel caps, and polishing the endless fenders of Lincolns and Mercuries and other fancy cars of the era. Not yet old enough to drive, maybe even misleading his boss about his age, he would move these enormous cars in and out of the workshop, careful not to make a scratch. When he wasn't in school, he worked. He decided not to be a stranger to hard work because it gave him the opportunities he envisioned along the way. And for the next two years, he continued to look for those opportunities until one day he fatefully walked into a grocery store—an A&P grocery store, to be exact. That was the day his world would change and his future life path would become clear—whether or not he knew it at the time.

My dad was just fifteen years old. How did **courage** play a role in his becoming a grocer? Well, at the time, you had to be sixteen to get a job at a grocery store, so when he entered the store to inquire about a job, he took the chance to act a bit older than he was, and he got the position. He would spend the next three years, or a few thousand hours, unloading delivery trucks, trimming lettuce, displaying fruits and vegetables, and training to become the best produce manager A&P had ever seen. By the time he was eighteen, he knew just about all there was to know about how a grocery store was run, and that knowledge would serve him well in the coming years.

The gumption and **courage** that led Stan to take jobs well before his peers did also drove him to take on other challenges. He decided to join, rather than be drafted into, the Marine Corps. Back then, very few people from his neck of the woods went to college. The draft was in effect, and most just went from high school to the workforce or took their chances with the armed forces. Dad was different; he was not only unconventional, he was courageous. In fact, he tried to enlist when he was just seventeen, a year shy of the age requirement, so he needed his mother to sign a waiver. Nothing doing there. Eventually, however, he would get his way, and on his eighteenth birthday he gave his mother a hug, shook his father's hand, and headed off to Parris Island as a new recruit. The Few. The Proud. The Marines. My dad.

Though he already knew something about hard work and

courage, nothing prepared him for being a newbie in the most feared fighting force the world has ever known. Stanley Walter Rusniaczyk, a brave, young eighteen-year-old from Cleveland, willingly left the safety of his hometown neighborhood with nothing but a small suitcase, his enlistment papers, and the fond memories of his childhood sweetheart, Ginger. Along with his good friend Kenny, Stan boarded a train and headed south, not knowing much about the path upon which they had just embarked. Reality came quickly.

My father was accustomed to lifting weights, and he and his buddy thought they were in pretty good shape. They soon learned that the physical strength required in the military paled in comparison to the mental strength that was required as a marine. It's a goal of the marines to separate the thinkers who thrive under pressure from those who buckle—and their methods were extremely effective. *Talk about hard work.* Imagine running several miles in the heat with an eighty-pound pack on your back, then standing still in the hot sun covered in sand fleas that bite like yellow jackets—and not being able to move. Not even a wince was allowed. Move one iota and pay the price of additional hard labor for the rest of the day. Or how about this part of the training: crawling on your belly through a wet, murky field with barbed wire inches from your head and a fifty-caliber machine gun spraying live rounds across the entire field? Lose your mind, even for a second, stand up, and you're dead. Can you imagine being eighteen years old and required to muster that strength and **courage**? And yet, right now, somewhere in this country, thousands of kids are doing just that. And more appreciation, I could not have.

Dad and Kenny endured two years of this treatment before they were honorably discharged in August of 1956. It wasn't all torture. Dad had some weekends off to visit Ginger, spend some time with her, and talk about their future together. They were soon engaged. While he was away, she planned their wedding and waited for him to come home safely. They married just six weeks after his discharge and moved into her mother's attic.

Shortly after his return, he returned to work at A&P. Older, wiser, tougher, and more confident in his abilities, and used to doing things with precision, Dad set out to create the best produce department in the entire company. Over the next few years, he moved on up within several different companies, taking a variety of jobs in the grocery business, and eventually landing at Kroger. By the time he was twenty-two, he realized he had higher aspirations than the produce department. Over the next several months, he proved himself by immersing himself in other departments and learned all he could. Never having had a road map to success, he relied upon the *courage* he had developed all his young life. Soon the corporate office began sending their new store manager trainees to Stan's Kroger for training. He would spend quality time with them, making sure they knew all the ins and outs of the various departments, including the benefits of colorful displays, proper lighting, customer enticements, and cost control. He began pumping out one successful store manager trainee after another.

It was at this point that the **courage** that kept nudging at him kicked in once again. He was ready to run an entire operation, and he knew it. He had proven to himself and his bosses that what he had learned from his four thousand hours of experience over the years could be used to create success in all the departments storewide. His time was now.

So off he went to the corporate office wearing the best suit and tie he could put together to meet with the upper executives and inquire about running his own store. To his surprise, he was flatly denied. When he pushed for the reason for such an abrupt denial, he was quickly informed that his *lack of a college degree* disqualified him for the job. Not one to take no for an answer, he went on, reminding them of his track record, and asked for an exception, but was told that there was no precedent to make such a request happen.

Now here comes the really courageous part. My dad knew his experience was qualification enough to handle the task of running a store. And so he did what I don't think many twenty-two-year-olds would have the gumption to do. He took a risk and simply laid it on the line. He looked the corporate guys in their eyes and said, "Wait a minute. You're telling me I can't be a store manager because of my lack of a college degree, and yet you are currently sending your new (and highly educated) store managers to ME to train! Please tell me how that makes sense."

Well, you might have guessed their reaction. *Solid blank stares*. And then this: a somewhat taken-aback executive making Stan a deal he couldn't refuse. He was told that he would be shipped to another store that was facing challenges in its produce department. "You go there, turn *that* place around, make it profitable, then we'll talk."

Challenge accepted, with the willingness to do what others wouldn't—in this case, to move to another city—Dad jumped at the chance to prove himself. He showed up at the troubled store and got straight to work. Six months later, he had built the most profitable produce department in Kroger's nationwide chain, and true to their corporate word, he was finally given the chance to run his own store.

At the time, there were more than eighty stores in the giant

Kroger Foods, and at twenty-three years of age, with no college degree, armed with nothing but a few thousand hours of experience, my dad became the youngest store manager in Kroger history. He also turned his store into one of the coolest shopping experiences around. Kids would get suckers while their moms shopped. Dads would get free beer and stand around telling stories while they waited. Yeah, this was THE place to be on a Saturday afternoon. And once again, Stan Rusniaczyk's efforts got noticed. His hard work, his creativity, and his perfect attention to detail created the type of success others wanted.

Over the next several years, he would work up to seventy hours a week in various capacities, succeeding in each new opportunity, eventually moving over to the business side. He worked hard to move up the corporate ladder, increasing his knowledge every day. At the same time, he was also able to avoid the typical pitfalls that came with big corporations—reorganizations, buyouts, mergers, and bankruptcies, which commonly took their toll on employees.

I can remember going to the office with him on Saturdays, as he often did just to check on things. As a young boy, I was super proud to walk those dark halls of his company on the way to his great big office. He was the owner of all things—phones, desks, file cabinets, AV equipment, not to mention a huge warehouse full of food samples from a hundred different product lines. I loved spending time there. Dad was the big boss, and I just thought that was so cool.

He remembers with shock, but also some pride, the time he was called to a meeting out of town. When he arrived, he was surprised to see all seventy-two regional sales managers in the room. The meeting was called to order, and, within a blink of an eye, sixty-two of them were sent packing. But not Dad. He survived that round of layoffs with a sense of accomplishment, yet that experience reinforced his drive to truly run his own show.

This is when he made his final move. Here is where **courage** came in once again. At just thirty-four, he decided to buy his first company, Smith, Weber & Swinton, Inc., a medium-sized food brokerage company that was being sold off by the current retiring president and his partner. The other owner soon retired too, along with a few junior partners, and Dad took the helm. His efforts expanded the company to sixty counties, covering some twelve hundred stores. In the process, he would make a name for himself and his company by quadrupling sales, attracting dozens of new accounts, acquiring competitors, and winning multiple national awards. He'd always known he had to work for himself, and now he had done it. Dad would spend the next twenty-plus years successfully running that company until he sold it in 1995 at the age of fifty-eight. He and Mom retired and now split their time between Ohio and Florida.

My dad always showed my brothers and me the value of hard work and the pursuit of perfection through attention to detail. Above all, he showed us what it means to be courageous. I will be forever grateful for all he has done for me and our entire family. He is the epitome of a man who possesses not only **courage**, but resilience, faith (Semper Fi), persistence, initiative, vision, simplicity, and generosity. The world would do well if it had a few more Stans in it.

So why have I decided to include **courage** as one of the cornerstones of a successful person? Because this characteristic is rooted in the history of our country, and it can differentiate those who have dreams from those who manage to accomplish them. From back in the 1800s when thousands of Scotsmen came to work in the Ohio and Pennsylvania coal mines, a truly courageous if not dangerous occupation, to the Irish iron-workers who stood on eight-inch beams two hundred feet in the air, to our modern-day ocean fishermen, **courage** is part of who we are.

And here is a secret: **courage** is in you as well. I promise you that. You just have to figure out what will bring it out in you, what you might want to do that would require **courage**, and then you'll have to find the strength to allow it to work for you.

5

THE CRISIS IN THE AMERICAN WORKFORCE

Now that we've learned a bit about the origins of *blue collar* and started to explain some of the attributes within it that will no doubt lead to your success, this chapter will provide a layout of the blue-collar landscape.

I call this chapter a **crisis** in the American workforce, but it is also an **opportunity**. It was an opportunity for me three decades ago, and it's even more of an opportunity for you today.

As you read this chapter, I'd like you to ask yourself one specific question: *What's in it for me to learn this information?* I need you to keep that question in front of your mind as you read because, as I said earlier, the whole purpose of this book is to give YOU what YOU need to make your comfort, peace, and freedom in life happen and happen now.

Here's the underlying idea: it has been proven that opportunity lies in the places where demand is the highest. Demand is the highest where the supply of a product, or in this case a service, is scarce. "I can't get that landscaper to call me back!" I am sure you have heard some version of that comment recently, am I right? So maybe it is time for you to stop focusing on what most people out there ARE doing and instead become keenly aware of what they AREN'T doing. Supply and demand are powerful forces, and my goal is to get you to see that you can take full advantage of that force.

And here's the final hint: this is also where all the money is! You see prices, or in this case wages you can earn, rise as supply falls or gets harder to find. The rarest gems are the most expensive. The last few plane seats are ridiculous, right? The same thing holds true with skills. As fewer people do them, wages rise. Pretty simple. And that means you can do what you are passionate about . . . and make an amazing living at the same time. What could be better than that?

However, before we get into the massive opportunity a blue-collar life represents, let's first discuss the crisis, since that is, after all, the title of this chapter. It's a crisis because the number of skilled blue-collar workers as a nation is shrinking by the day, while the demand from an ever-expanding economy is growing. According to ManpowerGroup, employers around the world are facing the most acute talent shortage since 2006, and of the almost forty thousand employers surveyed, 45 percent are struggling to fill roles, with skilled trades workers among the most difficult to find.* The situation is not improv-

---

* *"What Workers Want: 2019 Talent Shortage Survey,"* ManpowerGroup, https://go.manpowergroup.com/talent-shortage#thereport.

ing. A study by The Manufacturing Institute and Deloitte suggests a skills gap of two million workers over the next decade.[*]

What does "a skilled tradesperson" even mean? There is no official definition, although skilled tradespeople do share certain characteristics. *Skilled* is the operative word, so one criterion is that it is more than just routine labor. It's a skill learned and improved on over time in which you use your hands for something other than fingers on a keyboard. How much time? That's the best part. Most skills can initially be learned on the job in as little as a year or two. So that means you are getting PAID to learn, not the opposite. Novel idea, no? And while carpenters, electricians, plumbers, and welders are obvious examples, dozens of jobs are facing severe shortages, and I am willing to bet one of them could be something you would become passionate doing. Does working with your hands, maybe even for yourself, potentially outside in the fresh air versus being stuck in a four-by-four-foot cubicle on the fifth floor of some dull, aging building, appeal to you? Have I struck a chord yet? Let's get a bit deeper into this.

According to the US Department of Labor, as of July 2017 a record 6.8 million jobs that require skilled laborers were left unfilled.[†] The Conference Board, a hundred-year-old member-driven think tank, forecasts that an already tight labor market is likely to get even tighter, with the threat of labor shortages particularly critical in skilled blue-collar occupations. "To put it

---

[*] *"2018 Deloitte and the Manufacturing Institute Skills Gap and Future of Work Study," http://www.themanufacturinginstitute.org/~/media/E323C4D8F 75A470E8C96D7A07F0A14FB/DI_2018_Deloitte_MFI_skills_gap_FoW_study.pdf.*

[†] *Patrick Gillespie, "U.S. Has Record 6 Million Job Openings, Even as 6.8 Million Americans Are Looking for Jobs," CNN Money, June 6, 2017.*

bluntly," the Conference Board report states, "there are simply not enough people in the labor force willing to work blue-collar jobs."[*]

To a certain extent, shortages are regional. A 2017 study from the Georgetown University Center on Education and the Workforce found that between 1991 and 2015, twelve states, mostly in the Northeast, were especially hard hit. But real-world examples can be found all over the country. Superior Plumbing in Atlanta employs forty plumbers who earn about $90,000 per year, roughly 70 percent higher than the region's average. Owner Jay Cunningham says he could fill twenty more plumbing jobs immediately if he could find people with the right set of skills.

How is this possible? One important explanation for this shortage is that so many skilled tradespeople are aging out of the workforce. Right now, 53 percent of skilled trades workers are over the age of forty-five—about 10 percent higher than the average across all jobs. Rob Dietz, chief economist at the National Association of Home Builders, points out that the median age of a construction worker is over forty years old. Even new workers are aging, according to Bill Irwin, executive director of Carpenters International Training Fund. He says the average age of a carpentry apprentice is twenty-seven, but that the ideal age is nineteen. And these are just national numbers. Again, it's worse in certain parts of the country than others. In Connecticut, Rhode Island, New Jersey, and New Hampshire, more than 60 percent of the skilled trades labor force is forty-five or older. Other Northeastern states, including Delaware,

---

[*] Adriana Belmonte, "America Is Running Low on Blue-Collar Workers," Yahoo! Finance, December 31, 2018.

Maine, and New York, also have rapidly aging skilled trades workforces, as do Midwestern states like Illinois and Ohio.

It is estimated that for every skilled worker coming into the workforce, there are five who retire. The average age of members in the International Brotherhood of Electrical Workers is fifty-two, and fewer and fewer young people are coming in behind them to fill the gap fast enough to make up the difference. As mentioned earlier, a similar story could be told about carpenters, plumbers, and welders, although for some reason the scarcity of electricians is expected to be particularly severe. Of the twenty-one skilled trades professions identified by the Virginia Manufacturers Association, the oldest group in the US is electrical technicians, with 38 percent of jobs held by workers fifty-five years and older—even higher than within the union membership cited above. According to the National Electrical Contractors Association, seven thousand electricians come on board each year while more than ten thousand retire.

Another contributing factor to the crisis in the American workforce is that as skilled blue-collar workers retire, they often have no one to take over for them. As we have discussed, oftentimes a person came to this country in the nineteenth or early twentieth century with practical skills. He or she might have begun as a type of day laborer, then been permanently employed by a construction firm, only to branch out on their own to create a much-needed service business like plumbing, laundry, electrical, cleaning, or carpentry. They started doing the work themselves, hired other skilled workers as needed, and built a thriving business based on the quality of their work. They trained their sons or daughters to take over the business, who ultimately handed it over to the next generation, and so on. As a result, many of today's small skilled trades businesses

are second-, third-, or fourth-generation, and the current owners are finding that the next generation isn't nearly as interested
in keeping the company alive. Quick story on that before we
continue.

Consider the stonemason I hired to work on an outdoor
kitchen we were planning at our home. He was really good at
what he did and was extremely busy as a result. Often, his customers had to wait months to hire him. Because of his amazing
talent, we were all too willing to wait, and when he did finally
arrive, we were thrilled. Nancy and I couldn't wait to get the
project going. (There's that anticipation thing again.)

Coming from a construction background myself, I enjoyed
watching him and his crew do their thing—their dedication to
their craft, the comradery they shared, and the satisfaction they
all clearly felt after a good day's work. The owner of the company had a successful business, with more than half a dozen
craftsmen working for him who clearly loved what they did.
But while his workers were whistling as they set stone, I learned
the owner was considering shutting down his company. He was
ready to retire and had no family member who had expressed
interest in stonemasonry, and no employee with the business
acumen needed to run a large operation. Can you imagine the
lost opportunity here? Think for one second how the owner
of this thriving business must be feeling. Here he has built a
successful company over many years, acquired new trucks and
modern equipment, a great reputation, long-term relationships
with his customers, and more work than he can keep up with,
not to mention a salary of over $200K per year . . . and he can
find no one to step into his shoes. Amazing, no? For most of
his career, supply and demand worked well in his favor. In this
instance, however, it worked against him.

Just a bit more on this most powerful driver of economies. I have heard the phrase *supply and demand* many times, yet when it comes to its actual meaning, it can be confusing. To review, the simple definition is "the available amount or supply of goods and services as compared to the desire of the buyers for them." Popular companies you see on every street corner thrive on this most reliable set of economic laws. Fast-food restaurants, gas stations, and pharmacies know all too well how to position themselves to be right where you need them to be.

But for my purposes, I'm referring to a law of supply and demand that is related to the labor force, particularly the skilled trades—that is to say, the ever-shrinking number of workers in blue-collar fields, compared to the increasing number of customers who need their help. In this case, supply and demand is seriously out of whack. Ask any homeowner today about how difficult it is to find good-quality contractors to help maintain their homes and you'll get both frustration and laughter, as the industry is seriously struggling to keep up. The current situation is this:

1. Can you even find the tradespeople you need?
2. Are they any good at what they do?
3. How long are you willing to wait?

In my town, a home that once took six to eight months to build now takes well over a year, IF you can find a builder willing to commit to a start date. And this is not a temporary situation based on a temporarily good economy. The attrition rate of most tradespeople has been increasing for over a decade. Why? Well, consider this: according to Bill Stoller, CEO of Express Employment Professionals, one of the top staffing companies in North America, "For the first time in modern history, blue collar job openings outnumber white collar opportunities. . . . [It's] time to rethink negative stereotypes about blue collar work. Job seekers really are in the driver's seat, and that's part of the reason we are seeing rising wages in many of these fields."[*]

According to *Industry Week* magazine, these shortages are the result of "converging demographic, educational, and economic trends in the US economy."[†] Part of the problem is that older generations are retiring at rapid rates, leaving what I call "working gaps" in those trades. More important, though, is my conclusion over the years that our youth have been way oversold on the benefits of a four-year college degree. The job vs. degree balance pendulum has swung way too far in one direction. It's college or else, we're led to believe. As a result, we have stigmatized having a career in which one uses his or her hands. I've heard it myself when adults discuss their kids' career aspirations. As one parent laments to another, "Yeah, Cheryl's son . . . he's just a plumber." Crazy!

AMERICA SEARCHING FOR SOLUTIONS— WOMEN, TEENS, AND IN-COMPANY LEARNING

One way that blue-collar industries are trying to mitigate shortages of blue-collar workers is by recruiting women. The gender balance in blue-collar jobs is still not equal by any means, but it's improving. The US Bureau of Labor Statistics tells us that

[*] PR Newswire, *"The State of Blue Collar America: Satisfied with Work, Satisfied with Life,"* Oklahoma City, February 13, 2019.
[†] IW Staff, *"Blue-Collar Workers Are Now Scarcer than White-Collar Workers,"* Industry Week, *December 19, 2018.*

the percentage of women in the workforce has remained un-
changed over the last five years at 46.9 percent. But as usual,
statistics don't tell the whole story. In my experience, many
businesses around the country are making a real effort to at-
tract women to skilled trades, whether it's reaching out to high
schools, Sunday schools, or the Girl Scouts. More and more,
employers are also trying to offer flexible hours so moms (and
dads) can be with their children at school drop-off and pickup
times, or twelve-hour Saturday and Sunday shifts, which allow one parent to work on the weekend, when their spouse
can take care of the children. Some trucking companies have
initiated relays so women with children don't have to be on the
road for weeks at a time.

Another factor leading the increased number of women
in blue-collar jobs is that technology has in many cases made
brains more important than brawn, and we all know that
women are smarter than men. In Virginia, Barbara Gaskins is
the only woman in her seventeen-person rotation who operates
a CRMG cantilever, a seventy-foot-tall machine that reaches
over four sets of railroad tracks to load and unload trains and
trucks. Her team moves about five hundred boxes a day, including forty-foot containers weighing thirty tons. But Gaskins
does it all in an office, controlling the giant machine with two
joysticks and thirty buttons, watching her universe unfold on
about a dozen TV screens.

Women still face significant discrimination and harassment
in traditionally male-dominated jobs, and in some old-fashioned
circles, it's still frowned upon for women to get dirt under their
nails on a job site. But perceptions and attitudes are changing,
and women are holding a larger share of traditionally male-
dominated jobs, including construction workers, mechanics,

plumbers, electricians, highway maintenance workers, and truck drivers. According to the Bureau of Labor Statistics, as of 2018 women now make up 9.9 percent of construction workers nationally, up from 8.9 percent in 2014, and 24.4 percent of transportation and utilities workers, compared to 23 percent five years ago. That's a slow rise, but a move in the right direction. It's also good news for families, since blue-collar jobs pay significantly more than traditionally female jobs, such as entry-level restaurant or retail positions. It's also a win for employers, who are looking to alternative workforces to fill high-demand jobs that baby boomers are rapidly exiting due to retirement.

Still, there's a long way to go. At the port in Hampton Roads, which includes Newport News Marine Terminal, Norfolk International Terminals, Portsmouth Marine Terminal, and Virginia International Gateway, only 220 of the 2,400 longshorepeople responsible for loading, unloading, and inspecting cargo at local ports are women. But that's a start. A few decades ago the number was zero. One of these women is Shekida Green, who began as a laborer fifteen years ago and still operates a crane that loads and unloads rail cars, barges, trucks, and ships. She's also the first black woman to become a local president in the International Longshoremen's Association.

Local manufacturing companies are partnering with high schools to find workers to fill the skilled labor shortage, and increasingly are gender-blind in their hiring. In northeastern Pennsylvania, Erie High School junior Emma's dream is to become a welder, and she is learning the trade in shop class. Out of seventy-five students who study welding at the school, she is one of only three women in the program.

In addition to recruiting more women, local employees are

taking it upon themselves to fill their draining pipeline by beginning their recruitment early—at the very least, encouraging
high schools to teach practical skills and to sponsor apprentice-
ship programs. Remember when every high school offered
shop classes where students could learn how to hammer a nail,
weld a pipe, and fix a car? For many students, this was their first
exposure to the kind of hands-on experience that could ignite
a career in a trade. Just a few decades ago, our public education
system provided ample opportunities for young people to learn
about careers in manufacturing and other vocational trades.
Yet today, many high schools neglect teaching students about
the many paths vocational education can open.

Apprenticeships, on-the-job training, and vocational programs at community colleges are some ways young people can
learn, and learn to love, blue-collar skills. They don't require
expensive, four-year degrees for which many students are not
suited. Savvy businesses are demonstrating to prospective
employees that a skilled entry-level job in the construction
industry, for example, can be the start of a long-term, lucrative career. According to a 2019 report by the research arm of
the Commercial Real Estate Development Association, when
employees are aware of future opportunities for development
and advancement, they are less likely to treat a job as a short-
term arrangement and are more likely to invest in their own
skills. "Investment," according to the report, might include
something as simple as taking on-the-job training seriously,
but will also often mean enrolling in courses at a technical,
trade, or community school. The report also points out that
declining public-school focus on vocational education has
exacerbated a shortage of entry-level workers, and suggests

businesses need to do a better job of investing in the training and recruiting of high school students and recent high school graduates.[*]

I found another report particularly fascinating, this one a lengthy, detailed document published by the international consulting company Bain & Company, on what it calls career-connected learning (CCL). It reinforces many of the most important points I write about by describing the mismatch between the skills and experiences required to succeed in blue-collar jobs, and the education our students are receiving. I couldn't have said this better myself:

> *Attaining a four-year college degree immediately after high school will continue to be the right ambition for many young people. But a single-minded pursuit of college, absent related career experiences and a clear view of how that education will be put to use, is failing too many of our students.*
>
> *We need new pathways that combine classroom learning with meaningful, on-the-job work experiences that lead to door-opening post-secondary degrees and credentials. Well-designed CCL programs . . . [are] our best chance . . . to recommit to the idea that the American dream should be open to anyone willing to work for it. . . .*
>
> *Educators need to embrace the idea that a student who pursues a study-and-work path with her eyes set on both a good job and a degree is not on a less important path than*

---

[*] *Shawn Moura, PhD, "Finding Solutions to the Workforce Skills Gap in Construction and Logistics," NAIOP newsletter, Fall 2019 issue.*

*a student who is pursuing a study-then-work path straight
into a four-year academic-only program.*

The Bain Report defines a CCL system as one that brings
together all parties with a stake in career-connected learning,
including employers, K–12 educators, and state and local gov-
ernments. It's a win-win. These efforts can reinvigorate the
American dream for a new generation of young people, while
at the same time helping businesses access the talent and capa-
bilities they need.

The Bain Report points to a handful of states, notably Colorado, Delaware, Washington, and Wisconsin, that have had
great success with promoting CCL programs. But many other
communities are recognizing the value of blue-collar education in their own way. Michigan's Department of Talent and
Economic Development has launched a Going PRO campaign
to promote the professional trades. Its website lays it on the
line, pointing out that entry-level electrical power line installers and repairers earn $77,000, and plumbers and pipe fitters
earn $65,000. And Georgia recently spent $3 million on a campaign to promote its technical colleges. It's offering a tuition-
free grant program for seventeen high-demand jobs, including
commercial truck driving, electrical linemen, and diesel equipment technology.

Eight years ago, Hayden Bramlett was suffering through
business courses at Valdosta State University in South Georgia.

* Chris Bierly and Abigail Smith, "Making the Leap: How to Take the Promise of
Career-Connected Learning to Scale," Bain & Company, January 31, 2019, https://
www.bain.com/insights/making-the-leap-how-to-take-the-promise-of-career
-connected-learning-to-scale/.

"It was like watching paint dry," he told *Business Insider*. Today, the twenty-eight-year-old is completing a four-year electrician training program at an Independent Electrical Contractors campus in Atlanta. Meanwhile, he's working for one of the area's largest electrical, plumbing, and air-conditioning companies, in some years earning over $100,000.

SOCIAL PRESSURE STANDS IN THE WAY

So, while there is an ongoing crisis, there is clearly a lot of opportunity as well! The shortage of skilled blue-collar workers means that if you want to work doing what makes you happy, just go for it and you will find happiness. Don't take my word for it. According to last year's Harris poll of blue-collar workers, the vast majority—86 percent—are happy with their jobs, and 85 percent believe their lives are headed in the right direction.

One reason the current generation is avoiding the skilled trades is social pressure—the ludicrous idea that the only way to financial success is attending a four-year college and getting a job in an office. That thinking ignores the fact that there are millions of young people who don't want to spend their lives in a desk chair looking at a computer. In other words, the talent shortage is a direct result of societal and parental bias in favor of college over the trades. The absurdity of that attitude is a central thesis of this book. It ignores economic reality *and* the truism "Do what you love." Many people don't realize (or don't want to admit) that in this case, doing what you love can lead to financial success, or what I call "blue-collar cash."

If you are a high school graduate trying to decide what to do with your life, follow your heart. If you are a college graduate who can't seem to find a job in your field, be flexible, and don't be afraid to look for opportunity everywhere. If you are already years into the job market but are unhappy with what you are doing (and how your life path is progressing), use the law of supply and demand to help you discover what you are meant to do. Then, when you think you may have found the answer, be ready to take the plunge, to go where the opportunity is greatest. That's what Pete McGarity did. Listen to *his* story:

In 1998, Pete opened Headlines Barber Shop in Odessa, Texas. Business was steady but unspectacular, and he watched with interest as the nearby Permian Basin experienced a classic West Texas oil boom. The basin is an area of eighty-six thousand square miles that stretches from south of Lubbock to south of Midland and Odessa, all the way westward into southeastern New Mexico. Seemingly overnight, a gusher of crude production had transformed what was until a few years ago a remote stretch of scrubland and small, sleepy towns into a flourishing industrial zone employing hundreds of workers with high-paying jobs. Workers moved there because that's where the opportunity was. Pete also saw an opportunity.

In 2017, Pete scraped together enough money to turn an old, retrofitted trailer into a mobile barber shop. He drove it an hour west to Pecos, with the brilliant idea of parking it in front of the town's only grocery store, hoping to catch oil field workers between shifts. He hit the jackpot. His first day he started at noon and didn't stop cutting hair until after midnight. Today, he employs five barbers, who are busy all day long six days a week. They charge $40 a cut, a 60 percent increase from what Pete used to charge in Odessa. Patrons can move to the front of the line if they pay $60, or $75 when they also want a shave, which most do in large part due to their high wages and the need to take advantage of every precious and profitable overtime hour. Pete will personally earn about $180,000 in 2020 and is considering investing in more trailers that he'll send to other newly sprung towns in different parts of the West Texas oil boom.

Pete McGarity, a man who earns a living with his hands, a man who wasn't afraid of hard work, saw the opportunity and used the simple law of supply and demand to grow a great business. He is enjoying a great life for himself and his family.

ROB THE PLUMBER

Here's another story that illustrates how to take advantage of the law of supply and demand, and how crucial it is to recognize opportunity when it comes your way.

I first met Rob the plumber several years ago when he did some extensive plumbing work during the construction of our home. As the weeks went by, I got to know him pretty well. I learned that he'd come to plumbing somewhat serendipitously. His neighbor had decided to launch his own plumbing company, and Rob watched him as he started the company with two vans and then expanded it into a thriving business, twenty-two employees strong. Rob thought he could learn a thing or two from his neighbor. Not knowing much about plumbing, he jumped in with both feet and joined his neighbor's company. He figured he'd learn what he needed to know on the job. And that he did. A few years later, he decided to join a bigger firm, which specialized in new-construction plumbing. That was the company I hired to work on my project.

While Rob worked in my basement, we spent a lot of time

talking, and a relationship developed (as it does when you are talking about such personal things as toilet placements and sewer lines). Inevitably, the conversation turned from plumbing to my own occupation and how I run my business. I remember him asking a lot of questions. It was almost like he was contemplating starting a company of his own and that I was a sounding board of sorts, and I was only too happy to oblige. We often talked about the spirit and freedom of entrepreneurship, as well as, of course, about the financial rewards. It was at that point that I just flat-out asked him the question, "Hey, Rob, you thinking of going out on your own?" He told me that due to the demand for his type of service, and the inadequate supply he was seeing, that yes, he had thought about it a lot in recent months and had been talking to others about the idea as well, and was now just trying to find a way to pull the trigger.

You see, Rob and I had quite a bit in common. Neither of us had any formal training in creating a company, and neither of us early in our careers had any experience building teams of employees, the kind of experience needed to start a successful business. So it seemed we were there in my basement all those days just trying to figure it out.

During most of those impromptu discussions, we agreed that the most important ingredient was to recognize an opportunity that needed filling, then take a chance and work hard at it until it actually *worked*. We would recall how each of us had spent our early years working for someone else, just grinding it out and learning what we could along the way. And although at the time I was much further along in my career than he was, we developed a special kinship in our talks.

It wasn't long before Rob decided to open his own business. He knew the time had come. He had already spent several thousand hours in his profession, working the jobs, learning all he could, and he was now ready to run his own show. He called his new company C and R Plumbing. My small contribution was his first vehicle, an old van of mine with more than 200,000 miles on the odometer. And off he went, fixing drains, installing new faucets, updating the pipes. He was on his own, he was in demand, and he loved it.

About a year later, I would run into him again. Only this time, he was driving a brand-new Ford commercial van. His plumbing business was thriving. He was still using that old beater I had given him, but one of his employees was driving it now. Rob seemed extremely content in his newfound venture, and more customers and more vans followed—four in all—allowing C and R Plumbing to grow and prosper. Rob the plumber is a success story that we all can emulate. He had characteristics that exist in *all of us*: the ability to work hard and to put in the time, and a vision of the life he wanted. And most important, he had the commitment to see it all through. Supply and demand ruled once again.

What Rob did is not impossible to achieve. In fact, quite the opposite. In the book *Outliers*, Malcolm Gladwell argues that ten thousand hours is the magic number of greatness. Other researchers have attempted to debunk this idea, arguing that other factors, like age, intelligence, and talent, also play an important role. Of course they do, but in my experience Gladwell's thesis has a lot of validity. After all, practice makes perfect, or at least *more* perfect. Remember, we're talking about acquiring a skill to create a great living for yourself . . . not searching for the next Gretzky.

Gladwell's premise is that you can become great at anything if you're willing to put in the time practicing and learning for a measurable length of time. This, I am sure, seems like an eternity to a young person, but I beg to differ. If you were to work at a job forty hours a week, it would take you just five years to master whatever it is you're doing enough to go out on your own. It's simple math: forty hours a week is two thousand hours per year and that equals ten thousand hours in just five years. Your boss may not want you to know this, but it's true. It's a five-year path with several thousand steps, but it is clearly defined, with a beginning and an end. You can do this, and you know it. You just must be persistent. The difference between a novice and an expert is just ten thousand hours.

That's it. Stick with it, whatever *it* is you're doing, and see how great you can become. In your first hour, start with high integrity and keep it there for every other hour. Do you deliver on time? For a fair price? Do your clients trust you? Do people recommend you to their friends? If the answer to those questions is yes, then it is time to start your own company and live the life you dream of.

In the introduction, I mentioned that I wrote this book not just to point out the serious shortage of skilled tradespeople in the United States, but more important, to announce what this means for millions of talented, driven people, young or old, who find themselves in a similar situation as I did thirty years ago.

What does this shortage mean? It means that if you are talented with your hands, if you have a skill whereby you can make something or fix something, you have a valuable skill that can take you to tremendous heights. The message is simple. Be a carpenter! Be a welder! Be an electrician! Be a barber! But definitely be what you want to be, not what society expects you to be.

6

THE REALITY OF COLLEGE IN AMERICA

In the previous chapter, we described how the lack of skilled tradespeople has created an opportunity for those who seek a life of comfort, peace, and economic freedom by choosing to work with their hands. This has historically been shown to be a profitable choice in today's economy, and promises to remain one for years to come. I think most of us would be shocked to learn of the myriad blue-collar jobs available right now that pay seventy, eighty, ninety, even one hundred thousand dollars and more per year.

Now let's take a look at the other side—the employment reality for recent college graduates, most of whom are entering the real world with substantial (and many times shocking) debt. Studies have shown that average debt is currently

around $40,000 and climbing rapidly.* Most graduates start out
looking forward to finding their dream job in order to begin
their careers, but they are suddenly confronted with the sobering reality of paying off their loans. In *that* real world, college
graduates face both good news and bad. On one hand, those
who graduated during the past few years entered a job market
with rising starting salaries and an unemployment rate of less
than 4 percent, the lowest in almost two decades. On the other
hand, the latest surveys from a host of government and nonprofit agencies tell a slightly different story about the reality of
graduating from a four-year college and finding employment in
your chosen field.

Not surprising, over 70 percent of those in their last years
of college consider salary to be the most important consideration for postgraduate employment, according to LendEDU, a
financial site that serves as a marketplace for student loans and
credit cards.† Unfortunately, their research also suggests that
most graduates might be disappointed. While four of ten expect starting annual salaries of more than $60,000, and 17 per-
cent more than $80,000, that optimism doesn't mesh too well
with reality. The Hay Group, a division of the global consulting
company Korn Ferry, analyzed salary data for 310,000 entry-
level positions from over 1,000 organizations and concluded
that last year's college grads were due to earn an average salary
of just over $50,000.‡ In real dollars, that's two to six hundred

* Zack Friedman, "Student Loan Debt Statistics in 2019: A $1.5 Trillion Crisis,"
 Forbes, February 25, 2019.
† Mike Brown, "LendEDU's Class of 2017 Career Report," LendEDU, June 7, 2017,
 https://lendedu.com/blog/class-2017-career-report.
‡ "High Demand, Low Reward: Salaries for 2018 College Graduates Flat, Korn Ferry
 Analysis Shows," May 14, 2018, https://www.kornferry.com/press/high-demand
 -low-reward-salaries-for-2018-college-graduates-flat-korn-ferry-analysis-shows.

bucks per week lighter than expected, which could represent a car payment, or even a house payment. In other words, when matched with expectations, at least half of college graduates will receive salaries that are significantly lower than what they had originally anticipated.

But there's more. A variety of studies* suggest that more than half of college graduates are taking jobs that do not require a college degree, and according to the Bureau of Labor Statistics, less than 20 percent of American jobs require a bachelor's degree. Apple CEO Tim Cook recently confirmed this fact when he spoke of the "mismatch" between the skills people are acquiring in college and the ones demanded by modern businesses.† He noted that about half of Apple's new hires in 2018 did not have a four-year degree. Yes, you heard that right: 50 percent got in without a diploma.

The starting salaries for recent graduates have also stagnated. After adjusting for inflation, their median earnings were no higher in 2018 than they were in 2000 and 1990. What's more, according to the latest analysis from the New York Federal Reserve Bank, the unemployment rate for recent grads at the end of 2018 was 3.7 percent, slightly below that of the overall labor force, which was 3.8 percent. That's the smallest difference seen since the New York Fed began analyzing data in this way thirty years ago.

The National Association of Colleges and Employers confirms these numbers in a different way. This year, employers plan to hire 1.3 percent fewer college graduates than they did

---

* Bill McCarthy, "By the Numbers: Is College Worth the Cost?" *Politifact*, September 5, 2019.
† Hua Hsu, "Student Debt Is Transforming the American Family," *The New Yorker*, September 9, 2019.

last year. And according to a recent study by the Economic Policy Institute,* one in ten graduates are underemployed, more than in 2007. *Underemployment* is a fancy economic term defined by the Bureau of Labor Statistics and others as being unemployed, working part-time but wanting to work full-time, or wanting a job but having given up actively seeking work in the last four weeks.

The bottom line? Unemployment and underemployment rates for young college graduates remain above their 2000 levels, substantially so in the case of underemployment rates, and more than half accepted jobs that don't require a college degree. Think about that for a second. What did their life look like after that long, expensive four-year path?

COST/BENEFIT ANALYSIS

Everyone, from every part of the globe, knows about the American dream—our national ethos that comes straight from the Declaration of Independence, which says that "all men are created equal" with the right to "Life, Liberty and the pursuit of Happiness." For most people, one element of happiness is no doubt their own definition of financial success, and the idea that the only path toward this is by way of a college degree has grown popular during the last few decades. In 2012, President Obama called a college degree an "economic imperative that every family in America has to be able to afford."

Having never graduated college myself and enjoying a com-

---

* *Elise Gould, Zane Mokhiber, and Julia Wolfe, "Class of 2019 College Edition Report," Economic Policy Institute, May 14, 2019.*

fortable, peaceful, and financially free life, and knowing many people in the same boat (some in yachts, actually), I disagree with this idea. True, the pro-college movement is supported by data showing that those with a college education can earn more than those without. The Georgetown University Center on Education and the Workforce estimates that those holding a bachelor's degree will earn 74 percent more in median earnings during their lifetime than workers who stopped their education after high school.[*] And according to researchers Michael Greenstone and Adam Looney, an investment in a college degree delivers an inflation-adjusted annual return of more than 15 percent, significantly larger than the historical return on stocks, bonds, gold, or real estate (all below 3 percent).[†] "If college were a stock," writes University of California, Berkeley, economist Dr. Enrico Moretti in his book, *The New Geography of Jobs*, "it would be the darling of Wall Street."[‡]

Well, let's hang on just a minute here. I find this popular thinking overblown, and some of the statistics just downright misleading. For one thing, I know many people, including myself, who have worked hard and achieved financial success without a college degree. A number of their stories are told in this book. These are people just like you and me, willing to work very hard to get what they want out of life. But my accounts, of course, are anecdotal. A closer look at the hard data helps support my thesis.

....

[*] *Bill McCarthy, "By the Numbers: Is College Worth the Cost?," Politifact, September 5, 2019.*

[†] *Brandon Busteed, "The Convincing and Confusing Value of College Explained,"* Forbes, *September 3, 2019.*

[‡] *Enrico Moretti,* The New Geography of Jobs *(Boston: Houghton Mifflin Harcourt, 2012).*

In the first place, while there has been the often overstated idea about college graduates earning more than those without a degree, many young people who start college drop out, often due to the high costs of remaining in school. For them, these same economists found that income disparity between drop-outs and those who didn't go to college at all is insignificant. The student debt they took on, however, is very real.

Remember the laws of supply and demand. They are irre-futable in their accuracy. Just think it through for a minute. If the supply of college graduates increases dramatically, as it has in recent years, it only makes sense that the demand for them will fall, and with it, the value of their skills. Now, if the supply of blue-collar workers falls in the same fashion, then demand will have to rise, and with it, wages. Markets are efficient; they are undeniable.

Additionally, it is also true that since 2000, the growth in the wage gap between high school and college graduates has ceased. On average, one of every four college graduates now earns no more than those with only a high school diploma. While nearly 30 percent of Americans without a high school di-ploma live in poverty, compared to 5 percent with a bachelor's degree, that may have nothing to do with a lack of education. In other wealthy developed countries, a lack of even a high school diploma increases the probability of poverty by less than 5 per-cent, so it may be more related to our social structures than to the benefits of higher education.[*]

All this conflicting data begs the most important question: Is college worth it? For some people, yes, of course it is. Those

[*] *Ellen Ruppel Shell, "College May Not Be Worth It Anymore,"* New York Times, *May 16, 2018.*

who graduate from Harvard, Yale, or pretty much any top school and go right to Wall Street or Silicon Valley may well become millionaires very quickly. But let's get real: that's a tiny minority, even if there are many millions of other students who financially benefit from college in a smaller way, as the statistics above indicate.

But college isn't free. This section is a cost/benefit analysis, so let's also look at the costs. According to LendEDU, the average price, including tuition and fees, room and board, books and supplies, and transportation is $50,900 for a private four-year not-for-profit college, $40,940 at a public four-year college for out-of-state students, and $25,290 for in-state students.* For our purposes, we'll take the average of these three figures— just over $39,000, or a total of $156,000 for four years. These numbers, while frightening, don't even take into account at least two other considerations. For one thing, they don't factor in that, according to the nonprofit Complete College America and the Department of Education, the average student spends six years in college, not four,† so that would make the true cost of college $234,000. These often-cited averages also don't include the opportunity cost of *not* working—both in terms of financial remuneration and the lost opportunity of work experience that would otherwise help young people build a career and find financial success.

Let's now perform two additional simple calculations. If you could have earned, say, a modest $35,000 a year working full-time, that's another $140,000 for four years and $220,000 for six.

---

* Dave Rathmanner, "Average Cost of College Statistics for 2019," LendEDU, March 7, 2018.
† Danielle Douglas-Gabriel, "Why So Many Students Are Spending Six Years Getting a College Degree," Washington Post, December 2, 2014.

Of course, you wouldn't have all that money in the bank, since you would have had to live off your salary, but you certainly could have started to save.

STUDENT DEBT

We've seen the benefits—a likely higher ultimate salary and the intellectual stimulation you gain from four years of hitting the books. And we've seen the real costs, *and* the conflicting data on whether a degree will land you your dream job. But so far, we've ignored the other side of the coin, or should I say coins: the debt students accumulate, a staggering $1.5 trillion currently owed by nearly forty-five million borrowers. It's the second-highest consumer debt category, behind only mortgage debt.[*] The average borrower owes $34,144, up 62 percent during the last ten years.[†] And according to the Pew Research Center, 7 percent of borrowers, representing a whopping 2.5 million people, had at least $100,000 in student loans.[‡] None of these numbers even include credit card debt or other loans taken out for education.

There's another way to look at this too. The average monthly student loan payment for borrowers twenty to thirty years old is $351, so let's take that figure as a savings goal. If instead of paying off a monthly loan, you invested that same $351 in a modest 2 percent fund for ten years, you'd have a bank account of

[*] *Jessica Dickler, "Student Loan Balances Jump Nearly 150 Percent in a Decade," CNBC, August 29, 2019, https://www.cnbc.com/2017/08/29/student-loan-balances-jump-nearly-150-percent-in-a-decade.html.*

[†] *Zack Friedman, "Student Loan Debt Statistics in 2019: A $1.5 Trillion Crisis," Forbes, February 25, 2019.*

[‡] *Anthony Cilluffo, "5 Facts About Student Loans," Pew Research Center, August 13, 2019.*

$50,000 that you could use to buy a car, put a down payment on a home, or start a business. Those are other opportunities lost.

An increasing number of young people are recognizing that attending college is *not* a no-brainer. According to a report by NerdWallet, which has eighty or so "nerds" on its payroll to help consumers make sense of complicated money questions, nearly four in ten recent graduates don't think it's likely they'll be able to pay off their student loan debt within ten years.[*] Many also say that their student loans will impact their long-term plans to buy a home, get married, and have children. I think this fact should be the most concerning to us all. College was supposed to launch us into our eagerly envisioned life, not potentially hamstring it. And yet now Pew Research reports that about a third of student loan holders have come to the difficult conclusion that the lifetime financial costs of their bachelor's degree outweigh the very benefits that they went there to seek.[†]

I'm not alone, of course, in my belief that college is not for everyone. In economist Bryan Caplan's 2018 book, *The Case Against Education: Why the Education System Is a Waste of Time and Money*, he states his thesis pretty clearly in his title.[‡] For anthropologist Caitlin Zaloom's more recent book, *Indebted: How Families Make College Work at Any Cost*,[§] she interviewed dozens of students and their parents and concluded that an entire generation is coming of age with a financial and psychological indebtedness that will shadow them for much of their adult lives and

[*] *Elizabeth Renter, "Class of 2018 Money Outlook," NerdWallet, April 19, 2018.*

[†] *Anthony Cilluffo, "5 Facts About Student Loans," Pew Research Center, August 13, 2019.*

[‡] *Bryan Caplan,* The Case Against Education: Why the Education System Is a Waste of Time and Money *(Princeton, NJ: Princeton University Press, 2018).*

[§] *Caitlin Zaloom,* Indebted: How Families Make College Work at Any Cost *(Princeton, NJ: Princeton University Press, 2019).*

impede their transition toward self-sufficiency. This is disturbing, to say the least. More than one parent Zaloom interviewed only half-jokingly assured her that if their child's student loans couldn't be repaid, they had a backup plan—to win the lottery. The situation even once became the subject of television satire. Recently, truTV began airing *Paid Off*, a game show where contestants compete to get their student debt erased. Can you even imagine how that show came to be? When a situation becomes a reality show, it surely must be a problem.

COLLEGE ALTERNATIVES

Perhaps we can agree that college is great for some people, but not for everyone. That's why there's been an explosion of alternatives in recent years. If you already know you're talented in carpentry or electrical work or any other job where you use your hands, not much is stopping you from starting a home business immediately. Or if you already have found your passion, whether it's fixing or building things or soldering two pieces of metal together, but you know you need more training, you can refine your skills at a community or technical college, which will allow you to do what you love, rather than take courses that don't interest you and will be forgotten minutes after the final exam. For those of you in that situation, look for learning experiences that will prepare you for making a living at what you already enjoy and are practicing. In this tight labor market, you might also get on-the-job technical training after being hired for a spot that didn't initially require a college degree. Amazon recently announced it will be spending $700 million to retrain about a third of its workforce to improve the technical expertise of its entry-level coders and data technicians.

Internships are another way to get started. For many people, apprenticeships are even better, since you typically will be paid while getting on-the-job training from experienced professionals. Or if you have a great business idea but aren't convinced that a four-year college will help you achieve your goals, look around for an appropriate fellowship. Search the web for something that might suit you. PayPal founder Peter Thiel, for example, has established the Thiel Fellowship, which offers $100,000 to twenty young people each year to skip college and pursue a business idea while being mentored by the foundation's network of founders, investors, and scientists. The Fellowship website declares that "College can be good for learning about what's been done before, but it can also discourage you from doing something new. . . . young people can succeed by thinking for themselves instead of following a traditional track and competing on old career tracks."[*] Amen, I say.

Remember that everyone's path is different. That is the true essence of living. This point was once again driven home to me after talking to a friend of mine, who told me that a few years ago he dropped off his daughter at Bennington College, an expensive liberal arts program in rural Vermont. After he and his wife got her settled, he asked her if there was anything else he could do for her before they left.

"Yeah, take me home," she said.

Three semesters and one transfer later, his daughter was

---

[*] *Thiel Fellowship, https://thielfellowship.org.*

still miserable. He finally told her he wouldn't keep paying tuition only to have her remain unhappy. They talked about alternatives and explored a variety of gap-year ideas. She ended up driving her seven-year-old Toyota Corolla 2,500 miles to Montana to volunteer on a US Senate campaign. She was eighteen; she had never been on a long road trip before or stayed in a hotel by herself. In the campaign office, she made herself indispensable, doing anything that needed to be done, whether it was photocopying, licking envelopes, or reminding the campaign manager of what time she had to leave for a meeting. When the candidate won the election, this young girl was offered a job in the DC office. Today, she is a well-paid consultant, specializing in "compliance"—helping congressional campaigns around the country comply with FEC (Federal Election Commission) rules and regulations.

Unless you are wholeheartedly committed to four years of studying in the hallowed halls of an institution of higher learning, and it is, of course, perfectly fine if you are, challenge your assumptions before signing up for four (or six) years of tuition and student debt. Ask yourself, do you really need a bachelor's degree to become a web designer, a coder, an esthetician, a winemaker, a personal trainer, or any of a multitude of other lucrative professions? The internet makes researching alternatives easier than ever before in history. You want to learn coding? Check out sites like Codecademy to learn about web development. Even *winemaking* has its own page on CareerBuilder.com.

Another alternative: more and more young people are choosing a gap year either before, or instead of, college. There are dozens of sites that focus on exactly that. Echoing Green, Enstitute, UnCollege, My World of Work, Projects Abroad, and

Gap Year Association are just a few of them. Gap years can also work for people at any stage of their life. The Peace Corps has no age limit. The Corporation for National and Community Service and the Conservation Corps are two other federal agencies that offer tremendous volunteer opportunities. Another resource is RightSkill, a partnership between CareerBuilder and Capella Learning Solutions that helps people gain in-demand skills through nondegree learning courses, then helps facilitate job interviews, connecting its students with employers looking for their skill set.

The possibilities in today's connected world are limitless. You want to travel overseas? Lattitude Global Volunteering offers placements in New Zealand, working outdoors or teaching. STA can arrange an Australian working-holiday visa and help place you in a job as a deckhand, a camp counselor, an environmental worker, or in a café. Maybe you want to teach English in China. You can easily find recruiters like EnglishTeacherChina.com and job listing sites like ESLCafe.com and SeriousTeachers.com that will direct you to pathways that could help you develop and figure out how you see yourself and your potential skill set. And just maybe that gap-year experience (whether it is one of these experiences or just entering the job market) could go a long way to help you gain more clarity on just what you want your life to look like.

The final alternative—and, of course, in my mind, the best one—is that if you're good with your hands and are passionate about a particular skill, start with performing those skills for neighbors and friends. You'd be amazed just how quickly that can turn into a highly profitable business. More on that in the next section.

I was once asked to do a series of two-minute videos on various topics having to do with the blue-collar industry. In one of them, I was asked what I thought were the biggest areas of job opportunity and what skills were required. When the camera turned on and the producer said, "Action!" I raised my hands in front of me and waved them back and forth. "That's easy," I said. "Just about anything you can do with these!"

WORKING WITH YOUR HANDS, WITH PRIDE

"Handcrafted with Pride" are three words you see proudly stamped on a product when its creator is trying to convey the high quality or superior grade of their product or service. They may be the words you hear from a boutique owner, when the promise of excellent craftsmanship on that one-of-a-kind, must-have item is displayed. Think back to the last time you visited a farmers market or a street fair. You probably recognize some of these attributes:

- Handmade, with pride
- Hand-stitched leather
- Locally handcrafted
- Organically hand-dyed
- Hand-painted original
- Hand-cut and sawn
- Hand-polished

All these descriptions give the potential purchaser the impression that they could own something special because the given product was created with care, with pride, and with passion. It is something special, made by someone special, and chances are you will repeat these words to a friend or family member when describing it to them.

What do all these descriptions have in common? It's quite simple, actually—the four-letter word H-A-N-D. All these offerings were created by the labor of a single person, expertly handcrafted to ensure the best quality, the finest materials, and a promise of a product that will last for many years. Truth is, in today's society, working with your hands may be a slowly disappearing art, but that's not a negative, not for us. In fact, it bodes well for those considering entering into a skilled trade. Studies show that while the unemployment rate for all workers in the US is at a sixty-year low (as of early 2020 it was 3.6 percent), it may be even lower (or a negative number) for those willing to work with their most valuable appendages—their hands.*

You'll notice that I began this section with the word *PRIDE* in its title. What is pride? The dictionary defines it as "the pleasure or satisfaction derived from one's own achievements, closely associated with quality." Interesting. One might ask, how important is pride? And how does it relate to the blue-collar discussion? I call it the step-back reaction.

Imagine the stylist who spends a few hours painstakingly crafting a brand-new look for a nervous salon-goer, or the stonemason who builds an elegant gated entrance to a home, or even the florist who arranges a gorgeous bouquet for someone who is terribly ill. Or the artist who toils over the statue that will be placed in front of the local high school, or the farmer who wants to grow the perfect strawberry crop for the Saturday

---

* *Dana Wilkie, "The Blue-Collar Drought," Society for Human Resource Management, February 2, 2019, https://www.shrm.org/hr-today/news/all-things -work/pages/the-blue-collar-drought.aspx.*

morning farmers market. What do you think they all do when they have finally completed their craft, their task? I have been blessed to know these people and know them well, and I can tell you from firsthand experience that when it's time, they step back and gaze upon their efforts, filled with pride for the blood, sweat, and tears it took to get to that magical moment.

For centuries, great men and women have built America from the ground up, mostly with their bare hands. From nineteenth-century settlers to today's modern worker, one thing remains consistent, and that is our ability to put down whatever tool we used, wipe the sweat from our brow, and take a moment to revel in what we were called on to create. It is time to celebrate the blue-collar worker!

In that vein, I recently polled thousands of followers I have on Facebook, asking them to comment on the state of today's blue-collar work environment. I have seen some robust reactions to questions like these in the past, but they never compared to the enthusiasm, respect, and pride felt by those who responded to this inquiry. Here's just a sampling of the hundreds of responses received:

- Jody from Michigan—"Stick with it, be proud of what you do, always have integrity. I've been a carpenter for 25 years and absolutely love what I do. Every day is a new adventure."
- Cheryl from Mississippi—"Blue-Collar built this country. No shame in starting out without thousands in debt to make as much as we Blue-Collar folks do."
- Bob from North Carolina—"Do what you love, don't be afraid to go your own way, master your craft, and never forget those who helped you along the way."

- Joshua from Iowa—"Be prepared to get your hands dirty, to listen, and to do whatever you can to learn. Keep an open mind and adapt."
- Ed from Virginia—"Who do you think receives more desperate (and lucrative) phone calls, a philosophy major or a plumber?"
- Sam from Kentucky—"Pick a trade, there's nothing wrong with working with your hands. All trades are needing workers to replace all of us who are beginning to reach retirement age."
- Linda from Texas—"Learn the glass business. There is a shortage of competent glaziers!"
- Andrew from Illinois—"Working with your hands relieves stress, doesn't create it."
- Jack from Florida—"Pay close attention to the older folks. They can teach you ways that are a lot easier to do certain jobs, especially in the crafts and trades. They are in these high-paying jobs for a reason, plus quality and pride you can take along the way . . . especially if you have an interest in working for yourself."

There were many dozens more responses along these same lines. It happens to be the most reacted-to topic on my site and consistently draws the most likes, comments, and shares. I believe our creator gave us these amazing appendages for a reason. To use them. To build, to plant, to beautify, to repair, to hold, to love, to create music, and on and on.

You can tell by the comments that blue-collar careers are alive and well in this great nation, and I couldn't agree more. There are hundreds of articles, blogs, and other posts available with a click of the mouse that speak to the benefits of working with one's hands, and there has never been a better time to enter that category. Supply-and-demand curves almost always influence price, and as we saw in the previous chapter, with a serious shortage of workers willing to "dig in," literally and figuratively, the paychecks of these individuals have never been better—something you should take advantage of to get your life on track.

Our bottom line: careers that involve working with your hands, also known as blue-collar careers, are fueling the life plans of millions of people across the globe who are willing to see the forest through the trees. Remember this: I've always held the belief that we should plan our careers to support the vision of life we want for ourselves, not the other way around.

AIN'T NO SHAME IN IT

I'm not going to spend a lot of time on this, but it does need to be mentioned. I have heard on a few occasions that the lack of a college degree can be a source of despair or even shame—feeling looked down upon for not having spent four more years of your life in school and potentially racking up thousands in debt. To that I eloquently say, bullshit! There are many thousands of people who have achieved financial success without graduating college. In the second appendix of this book, there's a pretty impressive list of just a handful of them. The sheer number of them goes way beyond titans like Bill Gates, Mark Zuckerberg, and Lady Gaga. Though I've certainly not achieved the stratospheric success of those business titans, in a small way I'm one of them and can vouch for the idea that a bachelor's degree is not the only path that leads to fulfilling the American dream. Our Declaration of Independence guarantees the right to pursue happiness, not necessarily to achieve it. According to the US Census Bureau, just 33 percent of adults twenty-five and older have bachelor's degrees or higher, and you can't tell me that the other 67 percent are living in poverty. In fact, I can promise you that they are not.

Take a cue from psychologist Dr. Angela Lee Duckworth, author of *Grit: The Power of Passion and Perseverance*. She defines *grit* as "passion and perseverance for very long-term goals." She agrees that grit doesn't come from textbooks or exams, but rather from overcoming challenges in the real world and figuring out for yourself how to solve problems and make things work.[*]

Any of your passions can turn into a business, and in today's world, the cost of opening your own has never been lower. Unlike days of old (like ten years ago), in many cases you won't need start-up costs for rent, utilities, or even employees. All you'll need is a computer and the internet, which you no doubt already have.

INITIATIVE

The world is absolutely full of old and new opportunities to be taken advantage of. Young people who choose not to go to college instead have to think out of the box and take *initiative*, which, as we've mentioned, along with **vision, simplicity, faith, courage, humility, resilience, persistence, and generos-**

---

[*] *Angela Lee Duckworth,* Grit: The Power of Passion and Perseverance *(New York: Scribner, 2016).*

ity, are the characteristics of the blue-collar entrepreneur that will lead to blue-collar cash. Each of the people profiled in this book possesses one or more of them and will attest to their importance. Each of them made the *decision* to start something, and then *did* it. Easier said than done. How many of us go our whole lives saying, *someday* I am going to . . . ? Well, the difference between someone saying *someday* and saying *today* is that they possess *initiative*. They go out and, as Nike says, **just do it**.

Let's talk more about **initiative**. When I think of that character trait, I think of Arthur Hills. If you're a golfer, you may be familiar with the name. He has designed over 240 world-class golf courses in Mexico, Portugal, Canada, Sweden, Moscow, Japan, and the United States. How did this eighty-seven-year-old, world-renowned golf course designer get his start? How did he land that very first opportunity? Did he go to college for golf course design and then spend years working at a large firm as an underling, taking measurements and holding survey flags? Did he take the other conventional route of becoming a golf professional and then using his name and fame to put his ceremonial stamp on a new project?

Not even close.

So how then did this unconventional hero, who rose to legendary status in the golf world, get his first project, called Byrnwyck Country Club, now known as the famous Brandywine Country Club? He showed **initiative** by spending $17 for a tiny ad in the local newspaper, which simply read, *GOLF COURSE DESIGNER FOR HIRE*. I am not joking. *He just took out an ad*. He called himself a *golf course designer*. He let people know he was available for hire. That, my friends, is what we call *initiative*.

Sure, there's more to his story—namely the backstory of how a young man could develop the courage and **initiative** to put himself out there. Arthur Hills was born in 1932 in Toledo, Ohio, during the Depression. He grew up in the basement of his grandfather's house with his mother and father and seven siblings. His grandfather had been a well-to-do landowner until the Depression wiped him out. The family struggled to find their way. As a young man, Art worked at the greenhouse his mother's family had inherited until a family member ended his career and put him on the street. Like many teenagers just entering adulthood, he bounced around a bit. After serving in the army for a few years, he found work at a local garden center, doing small landscape jobs for a group of absentee owners. All the while, he knew he could do more. He wanted to sell the jobs, and design them, but though he was a hard worker, he had few sales skills, and little familiarity with the business.

One day one of the owners of the garden center stopped by to check in on the business. Art didn't think the owners had much knowledge about the bushes, trees, and plants that they offered, but this particular owner did know how to sell things. Art immediately understood he could learn from him. This man was willing to teach him all he knew about closing a deal.

After many hours of reading and discussing various sales techniques, Art was ready to use his newly learned skills and take on the landscape world. What was once, "Would you like a plant today?" was now replaced with, "And how many plants will you be needing today?" He learned to close a deal by asking, "Can I deliver those trees for you on Wednesday or Thursday?"

Now that Art had the sales skills to go along with his proficient plant knowledge, this budding landscape designer was armed and dangerous. He realized he just had to go after it and act like the job was already his. *He had to take **initiative**.*

About six months into his newly acquired effectiveness, he had sold a few tree-planting jobs which had not yet been installed when he received some bad news. The garden center was about to be shuttered. Out on the street again? Nope, not Art. With a small amount of borrowed money and a couple of worn-out trucks, Art convinced two of his former coworkers to take a chance and join him in a new enterprise. Art was open for business, selling flowers, planting trees, and raking mulch. He was thrilled to be his own boss and running his own show. Art recalls making $4,000 that year. "Not bad for my first year," he told me. He would go on to make $6,000 the next year, then $8,000, $12,500, $17,000, and finally $24,000. A sixfold increase in sales in just five years. Sixty years ago, this was good money, the equivalent of more than $200,000 today!

The entrepreneurial spirit that had helped Art get this far continued to burn deep inside of him. He knew there was more he wanted to do. The jobs were getting bigger and more complicated, but he knew he wanted to take his small landscaping company to the next level. With some experience under his belt, he had learned that installation was challenging and somewhat lucrative, but that the real money was in planning and design. So he decided that in his spare time he would enroll in adult learning classes in landscape architecture.

And then there came a point when fate stepped in, as it seems to do in many of the stories I share in this book. Very close to the college where Art took his classes was a golf course, where for twenty-six cents he could play a round of golf. Art was soon hooked on the game and started to think about how to merge his passion for golf and landscape design.

After taking a few informal design classes, in 1965, Art,

along with two Ohio State graduates, was landing landscape architect and site plan design projects. Soon, plans for large developments were on paper, and the small firm was busy landscaping entire neighborhoods and large commercial buildings. Art's business continued to grow, but he had another challenge. How could he remain busy year-round? Most landscaping firms shutter their businesses during the winter months and turn their trucks into snowplows to earn extra money. Winters can be tough in Ohio, and the right amount of snow can make you a small fortune if you are equipped to deal with it. But this wasn't Art's vision of what he wanted his company to be, so he asked his small design staff, "Fellas, what *else* can we do to survive the winter?" You see, Art was quite interested in what his team had to say. Then came a fateful answer: "How about we design golf courses?" You don't have to guess what Art's response was. He was game, and with that question, Arthur famously placed his simple $17 advertisement and launched what became a globally recognized business. Today, after designing over 240 golf courses around the world where most of us avid fans watch our favorite golfers play, Arthur is still on course.

Granted, times have changed, and most of us understand that putting an ad in a newspaper these days won't garner the same response. But Art's story can be a lesson for us all. Art decided what he wanted to do, and he went and did it. He had **initiative**. Imagine for a moment what you could do if you could place an ad today. What would it say? What could you offer? And then think of the steps you could take to do what Art did. Could you build a website? Take out a Facebook ad? Post flyers on telephone poles? You must start somewhere. Art did, and it worked out all right for him.

HUMILITY

I spoke earlier in this chapter about the ridiculous notion of feeling shame for not having a college degree. This shame likely stems from the feeling that you may be letting others down, e.g., your parents, your siblings, even your high school teachers. Nothing could be further from the truth. What matters most is what YOU want to do, not what others want you to do. Think about it. In this world, you owe it to one person, and one person only—YOU. Let me ask you this: Who but you knows who you are truly meant to be? Blue collar, white collar, whatever. Who but you knows what you are, or what you could really be good at? Who but you knows what passions live within you? Nuff said.

Finally, consider this story. It is a beautiful account of a life now rooted in **humility**, one of the character traits we have highlighted as essential to living the life you envision for yourself.

It involves a bright young lady I had the pleasure of meeting a few years back. Just for context, let's quickly define *humility*. **Humility** is a modest, conservative view of one's own importance—a humbleness. This definition will help you understand this woman's plight, and can help you on your own path as well.

I first met Natalia when she came into our office for an interview. My company was growing like crazy, and we had recently opened a new office to handle the demand from the new areas we had acquired to the south of our existing territory. Natalia came in to apply for a position in that new office. The first thing I noticed about her was an almost infectious energy.

A tall gal in her early twenties, she exuded confidence, looked you straight in the eye, and gave a firm handshake. She began to tell me her story of what had brought her to our office and her need for a job. After about twenty minutes of the usual interview conversation, she asked me about the job's hours and how strict I was about them. Unusual question, so I inquired as to what her concern was. It was then that she told me that she had been working for some time as an online brand ambassador. Obviously, I had no idea what that meant. When she explained her role to me, you could see her face just light up. I could quickly tell this was something she was passionate about, something she was meant to do. As I learned more about her successes thus far, and the upward trajectory of her online audience, we changed the subject away from a career in my office, sitting behind a desk, to what she obviously wanted as a career. There was no doubt in my mind, this is what she should be focusing on. And in an unusual twist of fate, we spent the next hour discussing how she would do just that.

Here's where the **humility** comes in. I had decided to stay in touch with her, as one never knows when you might need help navigating the marketing power of the internet. And she knew how to do that, to be sure. We had several other discussions, some even about this book. It was during one of these discussions that Natalia revealed why she had been looking for a job in the first place. She went on to tell me that she started her online personality back in her late teens. She would use a handheld camera and make short videos on anything from makeup application, to fashion trends, to dating advice, to the inner workings of modeling agencies and what to look out for. Soon she had a few hundred thousand followers! It was just a hobby, nothing she thought of as a career back then, and soon it became time to graduate from her small-town high school and attend college.

Smart as she was, it was decided she would attend medical school with the promise of becoming a doctor. How proud her parents must have been, and with good reason. "My daughter, the doctor." But something wasn't right.

Natalia went off to attend school in pursuit of a medical degree and was probably on target to amass a huge amount of debt in the process. A medical degree could have cost upward of two or three hundred thousand dollars. She was only in school for a few months when she decided she just didn't fit in. "This is not for me," she concluded. At around this same time, her internet audience continued to grow . . . now to more than five hundred thousand followers. Companies that needed their brands marketed came calling. She began charging a few thousand dollars for her videos promoting various products, makeup, clothing, etc. Soon her internet business was growing even while she was a full-time medical student. She was at a crossroads. She knew in her heart that internet marketing was where she was meant to be, yet how was she going to reconcile that dream with not having the medical degree that she and her family had always thought was so important? Can you imagine having to tell your family and friends that you are going to drop out of med school to become an internet marketing entrepreneur? Can you imagine the **humility** in that? But she did tell them, and she soon left med school and moved to California to grow her own brand, and her business. Today she has over 1.7 million followers. Her business continues to expand. Not only do brands pay handsomely for her to market their products, additional revenue comes from her participation on platforms like YouTube and Facebook.

CHOICES

For some reason, many people, especially young people, seem to be paralyzed by choices—whether to attend a four-year or community college or a trade school, take a gap year, or get started on an exciting blue-collar career right away. So many of us don't know what to do, or which path is the right one. And it's not only those of us who didn't go to college and are already in the workforce. According to *The Undecided College Student: An Academic and Career Advising Challenge*, the author, Virginia N. Gordon, PhD,[*] estimates that an average of 40 percent of students currently enrolled in colleges as freshmen begin school as "undecided" majors. That means millions of new students head off to school each year having absolutely no idea what it is they want to do in life. They're going to college because, well, it's "what they're supposed to do." Furthermore, of those who declare a major, a quarter of them will change it at some point during their first two years. And look at the number of people who enter professions or take jobs that have little to do with the degree they earned. According to the *Washington Post*,[†] only 27 percent of college graduates have a job related to their major, and according to a study conducted by the CareerBuilder job-recruiting website, 31 percent of all college-educated American workers age thirty-five or older never hold a job within their degree field.

This tells me a few things. First of all, we are sending kids to school who have no idea what to do with their lives. At the

[*] *Virginia Gordon,* The Undecided College Student: An Academic and Career Advising Challenge, *3rd ed. (Springfield, IL: Charles C Thomas Publisher, 2007).*
[†] *Zack Friedman, "Student Loan Debt Statistics in 2019: A $1.5 Trillion Crisis,"* Forbes, *February 25, 2019.*

same time, we are asking them to invest inordinate amounts of time, money, and resources into a degree that they may or may not want to receive and, more important, may or may not help them find a job after graduation—or, even more important than that, make them happy. *Talk about risky.* Not knowing what you want out of life or what you want to do doesn't come cheap— we saw that very clearly in the previous chapter. We know that according to the United States Federal Reserve website, Americans are now saddled by more student loan debt than ever. It's worth repeating the numbers. Approximately 45 million young Americans currently owe $1.5 trillion in student loan debt, and the average school loan owed by an individual is approximately $34,144 after graduation.

But even more disturbing than the financial cost of not knowing which path to choose is the *psychological cost* of not knowing—of spending a life unhappy, discontent, uncomfortable, and lacking peace or freedom. I, for one, think that cost is too high.

Ask yourself this right now: *How much is your life worth? How much are you willing to pay, financially or psychologically, for a life that you don't have a say in, don't want, or feel completely powerless to control?* I don't think young people, or anyone for that matter, should have to pay for a life they haven't chosen. Nobody deserves that result. You deserve to hear the truth. You deserve guidance, support, and helpful advice. You deserve to be shown alternative paths so that you can live the best possible life and, more important, give back to your community and country, which are in desperate need of your talents and services. For too long, the skilled labor industries have been ignored, to our country's detriment. Back in the eighties and nineties, our culture—movies, television, ads, and college admissions offices—were pushing higher education as the one and only way to make a go of it. And somehow that new mindset became so mainstream in the minds of Americans that if you *didn't* follow that path, you were likely looked down upon. Crazy, no?

Mechanics, farmers, seamstresses, factory workers, miners, construction workers, you name it, were, and sometimes still are, portrayed as people who just don't have "vision," or who are struggling to make ends meet. While this is a ridiculous conclusion, it is also the best-kept secret because the reality is that a lot of regular folks out there who make this country great work in jobs like these, and their work is no less fulfilling, satisfactory, and if done correctly, no less profitable than many other professions. Moreover, there are many ways to be successful, financially free, and even in some cases quite wealthy in these positions. In fact, the inevitable is occurring—the tremendous demand for skilled workers is slowly being recognized. That's true right now, and I suspect that the demand for boutique and niche industries where the supply is remarkably low today will in the next five to ten years only increase further. The moment in time when skilled laborer jobs were looked down upon was just that: a moment. It has passed, and that's a beautiful thing.

SO I'LL ASK THIS QUESTION AGAIN: WHO BUT YOU KNOWS WHAT YOU ARE TRULY meant to be? What could you be really good at? Does that have to begin with an expensive college degree, or are there alternative paths that can get you there? What would make your face light up? Who can YOU finally be?

7

THE BEAUTIFUL REALITY
OF THE BLUE-COLLAR LIFE:
A LESSON IN TIME

I am not exactly sure when the blue-collar career path lost its way in today's society. It seems as though it has been slowly moving in that direction for about a decade now—at least that's when I first noticed it. I believe the blue-collar industry suffered from a confluence of negative pressures that stem from multiple sources, all seeming to hit at the same time. The cultural push toward everyone attending college was certainly part of it. Also contributing, I think, was the onslaught of video games and the wildly popular handheld devices of the 2000s, which literally stole the attention span of our youth and dissuaded them from going outside and actually *doing* something. Not too long ago children actually spent their days playing outside in the yard or doing chores such as gardening or home maintenance projects, and this required them to actually pick up tools and learn how to use them. (Remember when every backyard had a hastily assembled tree house, built by the neighborhood kids?)

I was once asked what I thought was the best reason to choose to work in a blue-collar field, learning a skill and then using it to create a successful life. I remember giving my answer at the time, and it was all about the ability to control my own time. To this day, I look back at the realities of my four decades in the construction business and I can't help but smile, because my answer hasn't changed. I'll tell you this: the reality of a blue-collar life is beautiful, if for no other reason than that single word—*time*. Time. As you wander through life, you learn just how valuable a commodity time actually is. In this chapter I would like to share with you how I came to that conclusion in a somewhat dramatic fashion, and how the blue-collar life supports using time as your friend. I'd like to show you how to use this most valuable asset to your utmost advantage, especially when it comes to money, e.g., how time can work for you, how it can work against you, and why you should respect (and profit from) every single minute of it.

First, let's have a little fun. I am going to hit you with some interesting, some might call sobering, facts, so bear with me. The story I am about to tell you is true. It happened to me, and it sent me off on a journey of time appreciation. So here we go.

What if I told you, as an American you have an average life expectancy of 78.74 years?[*] If we were to break that number down further, it calculates to 28,740 days. Taking it one more

---

[*] H. Plecher, "*Life Expectancy in the United States 2017,*" *Statista, June 25, 2019.*

step, you would arrive at 690,220 hours and 5 minutes. Yep, that's your entire life pared down into tiny little pieces.

I can actually hear you asking the next obvious question: *So I wonder how much time I have left, and do I even want to know?*

Well, to get an accurate gauge of the number of days you have left to live, you're going to want to rerun the numbers after doing some subtracting. So do this quick calculation.

- Subtract whatever age you are now from 78.74.

  ....

- Got it? Okay, now multiply that number by 365, the number of days in a year: .... That's how many days you have left. Again, this is an average.
- It's even better to put this number into hours, which is easily done by multiplying the number of days you just arrived at by the number 24, which is hours in a day.

  ....

Got it? Good.

Now, if you are feeling a bit anxious or even a little depressed, never fear, you're gonna be fine. My intention with this exercise is not to create negative emotions in your fifth gallon. Actually, it is quite the opposite. The truth is, I've already experienced these particular emotions for you. Yes, I spent the better part of an Ohio winter doing just that—being acutely, painfully aware, if not even a bit saddened by this twisted bit of intel. As with most storm clouds, however, there was a silver lining. What I got out of the experience was a new lease on life, and a newfound respect for that most precious of all our possessions—time!

About twenty years ago, I was having what could only be described as a "rough go of it" during the winter season. Business had already slowed, so it meant that the upcoming "slow season" was going to be a very "lean season." You see, our company goal has always been to create enough work throughout the year to carry us through the winter until about March, the beginning of the new season, without laying off anyone during that difficult period. At times, this could be quite a challenge. Though I love what I do 99 percent of the time, I'll admit that sometimes it just sucks to be a business owner—especially when business is slow. I am very serious about my responsibility for keeping my staff employed and paid. I probably take it too personally. Needless to say, I was already heading into the holiday season stressed out.

I remember it was a cold, wintry day in late December. The annual holiday staff party was about to begin, a small gathering of just ten or so people who make up our management team. It was something of a potluck event, with each attendee bringing his or her favorite appetizer. It was a good day filled with funny stories of things that had happened throughout the year. The highlight of the afternoon was always the gift exchange, which was typically centered around gag gifts that would fill the room with belly laughs—something I could really use at that moment in time.

We gathered around my desk, gifts in hand, ready to start the exchange. Eventually, it came to my turn to receive, and I was handed a box about the size of a loaf of bread, along with the giver's customary sheepish grin. I gave the box a standard shake, then slowly and nervously began to unwrap it. Box now exposed, I saw the label written across the top: LIFE CLOCK.

"Life clock?" I asked.

The now-laughing staff member explained that it was a digital desk clock that tracked my life—or what was LEFT of my life—in hours, minutes, and seconds. *Hmm, interesting concept*, I thought quietly. Grateful, I thanked her for the gift and moved on. The festivities continued until all the gifts were opened and the last of the cheap champagne was gone. We said our goodbyes, gave each other a good hug, then locked up the doors, and went home to our families for the holiday weekend.

Little did I know how much my life was about to change because of that innocent-looking clock.

When I returned to work after the holidays, I thought, *What the heck: I'll set up the clock and see what it does.* It was a sleek-looking thing, long and narrow, shaped like a stealth bomber, and it had a cool, maroon swirl paint job. And so I wondered, *What could be so bad about knowing how much time I have left?*

So at the ripe old age of thirty-three, I put in all the necessary info needed to calculate my "time left." I took a deep breath and hit the RUN button. The clock lights went crazy for a minute, and then, there on the screen, the following numbers appeared:

376,680 (HOURS), 47 (MINUTES), 15 (SECONDS).

Damn.

There it was, my remaining life in a nutshell, albeit an electronic nutshell. I scanned the instructions to see if I had any other steps to complete. That seemed to be it. I gazed at the clock and saw that it was now running—running in reverse, that is. Seconds were ticking away, then minutes.

Wow, pretty cool machine, I thought. *What a great idea!*

And so I spent the rest of that day working, occasionally glancing over to see how long it was taking to do the particular task I happened to be spending time on at that moment. This process continued for the next few days, and I began to take stock of just how much time was flying by while I was returning phone calls, attending my various meetings, and doing all the other activities required to run my company.

The following Monday I went into work and noticed 168 hours were gone from when I had originally set up the clock. It hit me right then and there: *I couldn't reset this thing!* I was never getting those hours back. They were gone forever! A minor wave of panic came over me. *I have so much to do! Time is limited!*

Over the next few days, I started to pay attention to the time vampires in my day. *What meetings could I eliminate? How could I shorten those that were necessary? Who didn't I need to talk to? Which calls were most important? How much time should I spend on email? Did that silly meeting really take that long? Was that conversation really worth twenty-eight minutes of my life? Why am I taking so long to make this simple decision?*

Suddenly, I became amazed at the amount of time that can easily be squandered by individuals, even by entire companies if they aren't fully present, thinking and working in the now. I began to understand what my grandfather meant when he jokingly asked, "Who wants to live to be a hundred?" Then he answered his own question: "I'll tell ya! The guy who's ninety-nine!"

Time was running out! (Or at least I was much more aware that it was.) I began to see the preciousness of each moment, each interaction, and how much of my time is wasted on mindless tasks and meaningless drama. Several times a day I even caught myself "wasting time" by staring at the clock, watching the seconds tick away like a time bomb in an episode of *Mac-Gyver.* I realized that if I wanted to accomplish anything, I had to make some choices. I had to prioritize the daily activities in my life.

All was not well. Something started to turn. A worrying, nagging feeling followed me everywhere I went—it invaded my five-gallon bucket of a brain. All I could see were the bright red blinking lights flashing back at me. I remember more than once at day's end turning off the lights in my office and as I closed the door, taking one last look . . . only to see the ticking clock glowing at me in the dark. It was ominous, to say the least. If freedom is feeling liberated, I was feeling the opposite. I felt constrained and trapped by the concept of time.

Then one day I woke up and said, "I can't do it. I can't move."

The thought of getting out of bed and going to the office only to see my life counting down terrified me. Even in my dreams, I could imagine the clock ticking away like some sort of electronic Grim Reaper. I realized that instead of inspiring me, it was slowly but surely draining the life out of me—*Death by a thousand minutes.*

Like some sick horror show, I had to sit there and bear witness to my own mortality. It was also having an effect on everyone around me. No one at the office was happy. Like I said, it had already been a slow season, and now my new best friend, Existential Crisis, was accompanying me to work each day. The tension mounted. One morning, I arrived at the office and someone had drawn a crude crayon picture of the employee who had gifted me the clock. The rest of the staff were throwing tomatoes at her—LOL.

I look back on those days now, and I just have to laugh. Apparently, no one was happy with me being unhappy—or now having to work at an accelerated pace so that everything could be done quickly in order to "save time." Nor did anyone appreciate the paralyzing bouts of paranoia that overcame me.

I suffered from what is known as *analysis paralysis*. Sometimes I could barely do anything more than stare at the clock—aka my mortality. I couldn't pick up a pencil, read a report, or make a phone call without thinking about the time I had left.

Eventually, I decided the only thing I could do to get over this madness was to stop the clock. I'll admit I was scared, but determined. However, to my dismay, it had no off switch! My only choice was to get down on my hands and knees, crawl under my desk, and pull the plug. At last, the relief I was looking for was about to be mine! The so-called Life Clock would now be powerless to strip me of my precious time. Life would be good again!

Exhausted, I crawled out from under the desk, collapsed in my office chair, and fought off tears of relief. I wiped my brow and then reached for the quiet remains of the treacherous villain, which I had now renamed the Death Clock.

Oh my Lord, the Death Clock . . . It was still ticking. Oh, the humanity! A shiver went through me. How could this be? Was this an Edgar Allan Poe story? Stephen King? I had taken its power source! How was it still alive? Was it supernatural? I steadied myself and thought: *The battery backup! Those triple-As of terror!*

I TORE OPEN THE CLOCK'S UNDERBELLY AND RIPPED OUT ITS REMAINING LIFE, ONE Duracell at a time. Finally, the Death Clock was silent. The drama was over. I could breathe again. Victory in hand, I gathered its plastic remains, walked them down to the dumpster, and gave them a heave. I felt alive and waved goodbye while my nemesis went on its way, a one-way ticket to the nearest landfill. The fear melted from the staff's faces as they emerged from their hiding places. The four-week ordeal of watching my life disappear before my very eyes had come to an end.

Or had it?

As one might imagine, this experience has had a positive and lasting effect on me, and on my respect for ol' father time. For all the drama and the angst it brought me, I also learned some valuable lessons—lessons I still use in both my personal and professional lives (albeit in a less maniacal fashion than before). While I don't recommend owning a Death Clock, I do think everyone should experience at least a week in hyper-awareness of their own time spent. It can quickly put the daily activities of your life into perspective.

And the lesson for me? *Life is really, really short.* Time is precious. And it is powerful. A couple things to remember here. As you will soon learn, time can either work FOR you—in the case of financial matters and life planning, for example—or it can work AGAINST you, as in making mistakes with time management, hesitating when making decisions, and mismanaging risk versus reward analyses.

Ironically, this awareness (when taken in small doses) is remarkably freeing. When we realize life is short, we immediately have to make some crucial life decisions. Suddenly, vegging out on the couch and binge-watching entire seasons of *The Office* doesn't seem like such a great idea. Suddenly, griping endlessly about a job we hate doesn't seem like the most effective use of our time. Suddenly, we don't feel beholden to all those social obligations with couples we have nothing in common with. No, instead we find the courage to say: "No thanks, we're busy!" And then suddenly we are FREE to do whatever it is we truly want to do! Amazing concept. Only when we are aware of life's fleeting nature can we become more present and more attuned to not only what requires our attention, but what we truly want to do.

So how are you going to spend the remaining five hundred thousand, four hundred thousand, or three hundred thousand hours of your allotted six hundred thousand hours on this great planet? Okay, that might be too overwhelming to think about. This might be a better question: *How are you going to use the next twenty-four hours you've been given?* How much of that time do you have planned out for making that career change, working toward your goals, spending time with people you love and care about, and enjoying the comfort and peace you deserve? Doing anything else now seems like a huge waste of time, doesn't it? So does worrying about things beyond your control, rehashing past mistakes, sweating petty annoyances, holding old grudges. How is every minute of your day allotted? Do you enjoy any *free* moments? I mean *free* as in *self-reliant, self-determined,* and *liberated.*

Most of you by now have a pretty good idea of what it means to be *free.* A lot of us have come to think of it as the time we have off of work. "What do you do in your *free time*?" someone you just met might ask you. Fair enough. I get it. Who doesn't love their free time? I sure love mine. But what if I told you that *all* of your time could be *free,* because it would be yours and yours alone, because you controlled it, and you and only you were in charge of it? What if I told you your work could be the pathway to ultimate freedom? By being self-reliant and deter-mined in both your work and home life, you could set yourself up for the life of your dreams. *Imagine what freedom awaits you. Imagine what you could accomplish.*

BLUE-COLLAR FINANCE 101—
ESTABLISHING CREDIT, PAY YOURSELF FIRST

Okay, so hopefully by now you're paying attention to how you spend your TIME. You're trying not to waste too much of it. That's not to say you can't binge on a particularly great Netflix, Amazon, HBO, or broadcast television series, but at least now you're much more aware of what you're doing and the consequences of your actions.

What I'd like to do now is to show you how time can work FOR you. As we discussed, there are a few time-tested ways to take advantage of time when it comes to our personal finances. And your goal here is to put time on your side when it comes to your money. Tips like how to establish and use credit, the best way to create a home budget, and the power of saving early for retirement are all important aspects of living a life of C, P, and F. So let's talk about the best ways to accomplish those things.

One of the first things I discuss with every person who comes to work at my company is the state of their credit. In many cases, the conversation quickly arrives at the fact that (a) they have not established credit, or (b) they have, but are not using it properly. In the case of those who have not yet waded into the credit pool, one of the first conversations I have with them revolves around credit cards and how to use them. I usually recommend establishing credit through the smart use of credit cards. In fact, I encourage them to apply for one as soon as possible. Bear with me here. This is not a discussion of spending beyond your means or buying anything you cannot afford. And, of course, discipline is paramount here. But the reality is that if you ever want to finance a car or convince a bank to give you a mortgage, you're going to need a credit history. Until our world figures out another way to measure a buyer's trustworthiness, establishing credit is the only way to do it. It may seem counterintuitive, but you need credit to establish credit.

So how do you establish credit? I recommend beginning by opening up a retail credit card, because approval is relatively easy. Go to a store where you want to buy something and—even though you have the cash in hand—apply for a credit card. Sometimes the store will give you the option to pay the bill that same day, and I recommend doing that if possible. Others make you wait for the bill to come in the mail. If that's the case, when the bill arrives, pay it all off at once, immediately. In other words, do not charge the card for the purchase if you don't have the cash to pay for it. This is important. We are NOT borrowing money from the credit card company. We are simply using it as a way to let the credit world know we are responsible with money. Do this for a few months and, voilà, you are on your way to having credit.

But there is more to this plan. Once you have paid that retail card in full for a few months straight, apply for a second card, this one a low-interest Mastercard or Visa. Only use it for purchases you know you can pay off right away, so you're never paying interest. Think of using your credit card just like your debit card. . . . You can't spend what you don't have, period. Using this method, by the time you are ready to buy a house or a car, your credit rating will be stellar. The higher your credit score—hopefully in the seven- to eight-hundred range—the lower your interest rate will be when you go to make a major purchase.

Remember this quick spending lesson—spend only on

items that will create an aura of comfort, peace, and freedom, not regret, disillusionment, or foolishness. Never, ever waver from this.

I saw a neat, spontaneous-purchasing trick on TV once. It goes like this: If you aren't absolutely in love with your potential purchase, act like you bought it but then leave it at the store for safekeeping. If you miss it terribly in the next few days, you can always go and pick it up. If you don't, well, guess what? You didn't need it to begin with. So if you're not entirely sure you can (or should) afford something, follow this psychological test. You'll be amazed how your purchasing decisions will improve.

No effective financial conversation can be had without an honest discussion about interest. There are basically two types. For simplicity's sake, we'll call them good and bad interest. One can make you rich, the other can make you poor.

We'll start our discussion with the bad—actually, the worst—credit card interest, probably the single, most offensive of them all. The is the kind that works *against* you, not *for* you, because, by its very design, it wants to move into your financial house . . . and never leave.

Here's an example. For this exercise, I want you to think of interest as though you are renting money, not unlike you would rent tables for a party from a rental center. The tables aren't yours; you are essentially paying someone to borrow them for a while. You pay them rent for as long as you use the tables, correct? So what do you typically do when you are done with the party? If you're like most people, you return the rented tables as fast as you possibly can, usually the very next day. You don't just let them lie around in your garage, all the time racking up more rent charges, right? Of course not. So then the obvious question is: Why would you do that with your money? To be frank, it's not even *your* money to begin with. It's the bank's money; you're paying them to borrow it. And the rent charges on credit card money are astronomical. According to the American multinational personal finance company Credit Karma, the average interest charge for using credit card money is a whopping 16 percent, with some as high as 24–26 percent! Borrowing money at these rates means it would take years to pay off the balances. That's their goal. Like a relationship gone south, first they meet you, then they move in . . . and never leave. Seems silly, doesn't it?

So here we are—

Financial Planning Lesson Number One: Use credit cards only to build good credit. Pay them off immediately, same day if possible. Avoid the bad relationship, avoid renting other people's money at all costs . . . at least for now.

Now let's talk about the opposite of paying to rent other people's money. How about getting paid to rent *your* money to *them*? Now we're talking! It's called investment. You essentially lend your money to others, and in return they pay you for the privilege. There are many forms of investment, some riskier than others, and we will not be discussing them here. I want to focus on a very simple idea that takes some discipline to follow, but only in the very beginning. This idea has been around for quite some time, but it gained popularity when it was given a rather catchy name by someone working with world-famous financial guru Dave Ramsey. The idea is called Pay Yourself First.

So many times I have heard people say, "When I get a bit of extra money, I'm going to start a savings account for my retirement." Did you catch that? *When I get a bit of extra money.* This tells me several things about the person speaking, but for the sake of time, I will focus on only a few. First, barring any totally unforeseen financial windfall occurring, does the *when I get a bit of extra money* ever come? Seriously, in most cases, does extra money ever just show up, knock on the door, and say, *I'm here?* Of course not.

Second, and more important, this statement tells me that saving for retirement is either something the speaker isn't making a priority or something the person simply doesn't know how to execute. Later in this chapter, we are going to talk about household budgets, but I tell you this now because I can show you how easy it is to design your financial future, if you put it first in line as a priority. Talk about a path to long-lasting comfort, peace, and freedom. Having your financial endgame front and center in your mind, and having that puzzle solved early in life, is an amazing feeling. Trust me on this one. Given its importance, let's now talk about the how-to. Allow me to show you some examples.

Paying yourself first needs no definition. It's as simple as that. You get your paycheck on Friday, and before you pay a bill or spend a dime, you put a predetermined amount aside in a vehicle of saving. And here's the key. You put it in a place you cannot access. Okay, I can hear the groans already. But it's true. You should know that this method of building your future hurts only once, and that pain is only felt at the very start. I'll tell you why. I'd like you to think back to the first day you were interviewed for the job you currently have. Or if you are currently looking for a job, you can use this clever maneuver right away. At some point in the interview, the subject of salary will come up. When it does, I'd like you to follow this plan. Assume for the sake of this discussion that you are offered a yearly salary of, let's say, $40,000. I would like you to immediately say to yourself, "Wow, they are offering me $37,000, great!" What have you just done? It's simple. You just decided to base your new world on a salary that is actually $3,000 less than you will be earning. What you never had, you can never miss, get the point? You will base all your household expenditures, including an emergency fund, on the lesser amount. Within a week's time, you will get used to living on the $37K. This is critical because money has a way of warping our thought process. The more you make, the more you spend. It's an unfortunate but basic human behavior. But not for you. You will go to the payroll department on day one and ask them to deduct the extra money into an account that you cannot and will not access, for any reason. Over the years, I have had many of my employees give me their debit cards to lock up in my safe, just as a precaution. Funny but true. Funny but effective.

So now let's add the magical element of time to this conversation. Time is money and money is time, plain and simple. And here's where interest comes back into play. The good interest. The kind that works FOR you. Interest and time are your money's best friend. So who's ready to be a millionaire? I'm not kidding. In my organization, we have at least thirty budding millionaires. They are team members, mainly in their twenties and thirties, who put in a good day's work and go home each night confident in the knowledge that their retirement is covered. How did this happen, what magic are they relying on to fund their later years, and how is this possible? For one thing, they have learned that putting aside $50 each week at the start of your career is easier than you think. Most people fritter away that much each week without even realizing it. They go out to dinner a couple of times, buy a cup of overpriced coffee every day, or purchase clothes on impulse that they may never wear. How much do you think many people spend picking up a bottle of wine, a six-pack, fast food, or cigarettes on their way home from a long day at work? It adds up, believe me. Keep track for just a few weeks and you'll see what I mean.

If you're not a spendthrift and you still find yourself struggling to get by and want to tell me, "Yeah, easier said than done, I don't have fifty bucks a week," I am going to ask you to look closer at your spending habits. If you still can't put $50 away, can you manage $20? Or even $10? Then do that, and increase the amount as your salary increases. You have to be systematic about this. Never underestimate the power of time, interest, and money working in partnership to create the kind of lives dreams are made of.

And how about those young, ditch-digging, blue-collar millionaires? What retirement vehicle are they using? It's one of the best savings accounts going. I'm talking about the 401(k).

Most companies offer a 401(k) or another type of retirement-saving opportunity that allows you to easily deduct a certain amount each week from your pay. Inquire about them. A standard recommendation is to put 15 percent of your gross income toward retirement. If your employer offers a 401(k) account, particularly if it matches your contribution, take advantage of that opportunity in full. Pay close attention here. The 401(k) with employer match is one of the best savings games in town. Here's why. When you put money away into a standard bank savings account, you are saving *after-tax* money. You have a dollar to put away, but after taxes you are saving only about seventy-five cents. Still a good thing to do, but there are much better ways to accumulate a solid retirement. With a 401(k) account, the government allows you to save the dollar tax-free. So if you save a dollar to put in one of these accounts, it's a whole dollar versus seventy-five cents . . . meaning you are already up a quarter over a standard bank account. Good stuff, but it gets even better. Many companies also offer a match on what you save as a way of retaining good employees. This is usually about a quarter of what you save, up to a certain percentage of your income. Now here's the magic. You not only get to keep the tax-free quarter, but you also get a quarter from the company match. So for every dollar you save in a 401(k), you now have one dollar and a quarter versus the seventy-five cents—a fifty-cent swing in your direction. Pretty cool eh? Just think how much more in dollars you would have over many years. It's huge.

As you can probably tell, I'm a big fan of 401(k)s. I have had one in my company for many years, and it has created and will continue to create millionaires. Exactly how does this amazing result happen? Well, remember the formula for investing in your future . . . money, interest, and time. They are an unbelievable team. Here's how they work their magic for those willing to be disciplined enough to use them, especially if you start early in life. Saddle up: you aren't going to believe this.

THE POWER OF STARTING EARLY AND SAVING

Financial Planning Lesson Number Two: No matter how old you are now, at some point in your life you will likely want to retire. If you start planning for it when you're sixty-five, or even fifty-five or forty-five, you're basically screwed. So get started on retirement savings as soon as you start earning an income. It's best to learn this profitable habit in your twenties.

How much will you need to be able to retire? Take a guess. According to a recent study, six in ten Americans believe that when they retire, they'll need $1 million for a comfortable retirement.[*] Unfortunately, a Ramsey Solutions study reports that half of baby boomers, a generation that has had a long time to save, have saved less than $10,000.[†] It's not as if Americans don't know this is a crisis. Most people know they are way behind when it comes to saving for retirement. In fact, more than half of all working Americans admit that they lose sleep thinking about it. But not you, at least not after you read this book!

Saving for retirement may seem like hard work, but there's good news. You can do it, and you can do it easily. It's not, as they say, rocket science. Start saving now; it's as simple as that. The only way to create a comfortable nest egg is to start saving immediately and to allow the combination of your rising in-

---

[*] *"2019 Retirement Pulse Survey: Catching Up on Retirement Savings," Ameritrade, September 2019, https://s2.q4cdn.com/437609071/files/doc_news/research/2019/retirement-pulse-survey.pdf.*

[†] *Dave Ramsey, "Millennials and Retirement," June 15, 2016, https://www.daveramsey.com/research/millennials.*

come and compound growth to build your retirement fund for you. A fairy godmother is not going to be magically waiting for you with a pot of money when you retire. You've got to actually save it for yourself, and it's a lot easier than you think.

To give you an idea of the awesome power of the retirement team—money, interest, and time—let's compare two people of the same age: twenty-four-year-olds Jack and Jill, a riff on the comparison Dave Ramsey describes in the post *How Teens Can Become Millionaires* on his website.* Both are interested in saving for retirement, but Jill decides to start saving right away, while Jack procrastinates and puts it off for about ten years. Here's where it gets really interesting. I should mention that I am indebted to author and financial advisor Chris Hogan for this analysis (and you will be too). So back to Jack and Jill, our two young savers. Jill begins saving for retirement as soon as she starts working at her first job. At age twenty-four, she pays herself first and puts about $50 per week (with a company match of about $3,000 each year) into her 401(k) retirement account, and she does that for ten years. On her thirty-fifth birthday, she decides she has saved enough and stops. Nevertheless, with the company match and an annual rate of return of 6–10 percent, which is aggressive but happens to be the historical average return rate of the S&P 500, Jill will have a nice nest egg when she retires at sixty-five. Just how much? Wait for it . . . wait for it . . . First, we'll see how Jack does, and then we'll let you know.

Speaking of Jack, let's take a look at his situation. Jack, who again is the same age as Jill, begins his career at the same age,

* Dave Ramsey, "How Teens Can Become Millionaires," https://www.daveramsey.com /blog/how-teens-can-become-millionaires.

twenty-four. Remember that Jack puts off saving for retirement for the first ten years of his working life. Then after a decade of work, he realizes it is time, and he begins to save his own $3,000 every year and decides to do this for the next thirty years, versus Jill's ten. At sixty-five, they decide to compare notes to see how their investment accounts have grown. Jill, who started at age twenty-four, had an out-of-pocket cost of roughly $30,000 ($3,000 for ten years). Jack, who started at thirty-four, had an out-of-pocket cost of roughly $90,000 ($3,000 for 30 years). When he opened his statement, he is pleasantly surprised to learn that he had accumulated over $600,000. "Not bad, huh?" he proudly proclaims. And then it is Jill's turn. Remember, she had a ten-year saving head start on Jack. She opens her statement and is shocked to learn that even though she has saved the same amount each week as Jack, but for only ten years versus his thirty, she has ended up with a retirement account of over $1 million! Yes, I know . . . unbelievable, but true. Oh, the power of saving money, the magic of interest appreciation, and the undeniable force of time.

And now **Financial Planning Lesson Number Three:** Find a financial vehicle in which to invest your money. Consult a family member or friend in the investment business. Ask your employer about a 401(k) or similar plan. And do it as soon as possible!

HOUSEHOLD BUDGETS—THE
SLICING OF THE PIE

As you can see, planning a successful long-term savings account is not as difficult as you might think. And how you look at money is critical to your success. I want to be able to show you how to get the rest of your life moving through goal-setting so you can use your income to create the life you want. So it's a good idea to finish this chapter with a quick lesson on how to use your precious dollars wisely.

To this day, I still can't believe they don't teach this in school. It seems that credit cards are easy to get, but the knowledge of how they work and how to properly use them is nowhere to be found. I feel like I owe it to you to give you, at the very least, an example of how to spend your hard-earned money in order to increase your financial well-being. There are many examples out there to be sure. A quick search of the internet gives some varying ideas of just what your budget could (and should) look like. Different financial advisors have slightly different household budget categories and what percentage of your income you should allocate for each of them. I've pointed a lot of people to Dave's recommendations,[*] although these need to be adjusted once children come along. And unfortunately, many of you will have to add student loan payments.

- Saving—10 percent
- Giving—10 percent

---

[*] R. J. Weiss, CFP, "Dave Ramsey Recommended Household Budget Percentages (+ How to Determine Your Own)," The Ways to Wealth, https://www.thewaysto wealth.com/money-management/household-budget-percentages/.

- Food—10 to 15 percent
- Utilities—5 to 10 percent
- Housing costs—25 percent
- Transportation—10 percent
- Health—5 to 10 percent
- Insurance—10 to 25 percent
- Recreation—5 to 10 percent
- Personal spending—5 to 10 percent
- Miscellaneous—5 to 10 percent

Please note these are just recommended guidelines to help you see how you are allocating your money. You should take the time to set your own budget based on these guidelines. Only you can figure out what percentage you should use for each expenditure. Notice that Saving is the very first category. That is not by accident. It should be your first priority. Be relentless here. Remember, we are trying to create real comfort, peace, and freedom in your life. And that begins with setting up (and then not worrying about) your retirement.

Finally, **Financial Planning Lesson Number Four:** Get your financial house in order. Set up a simple budget and follow it to the letter.

Our grandparents used to use coffee cans with the words RENT, UTILITIES, and GROCERIES written on them, into which they stuffed dollar bills in order to save enough to meet their daily and weekly expenses. Nowadays, of course, we do the same thing on our smartphones, only digitally. But the same result of disciplined savings occurs. And this practice will change your financial life for the better.

FINANCIAL PLANNING SUMMARY

If you do take the simple advice in this chapter, you will no doubt set yourself up for financial security and the lifelong peace that comes with that. You will be disciplined with your money. You will never sweat your bills, and you will likely have enough money for anything you truly need. Every time you see a credit card bill with a zero balance, every time you see your savings account grow incrementally, you'll be empowered to keep going down the path to the life you envision. You'll be more confident, self-assured, and that five-gallon-bucket head of yours will be brimming with security, instead of worry, anxiety, and fear for the future. Best of all, you'll become a magnet for better and more amazing opportunities. You will be ready to take on that life drawing you so carefully created, one piece at a time. You will become a personal goal-crushing machine. You'll be unstoppable. Read on.

8

SETTING YOUR GOALS AND FOLLOWING THE RIGHT PATH

We have come to the point where we are ready to begin building your new life. Hopefully, you are now thinking better, seeing your potential future more clearly, reviewing your life plan drawing, and practicing better money management. Now we set our sights on setting up goals and achieving them, one by one.

If I could, I'd like to define the word *goal* (by now you know how much I love to define words to better understand them). So here we go. My distillation of the dictionary definition of *goal* is: *the object of a person's ambition, aim, or desired result, the destination of a journey.*

Interesting, no? Another way of saying this is . . . a goal is an *end*, an end that you see and focus on from the very *beginning*. You see the end from the very beginning. You begin with the end in mind. In Dr. Stephen R. Covey's amazing book *The 7 Habits of Highly Effective People,*[*] he discusses the process of goal-setting by writing that everything is essentially created twice, once in your mind's eye, and then once when it is physically made. I liken this thought process to a path. To take Dr. Covey's example, there are a multitude of steps that occur in the development of any goal, between what your mind first sees and when you create the actual physical thing. You will soon be hearing me talk a lot about paths—paths that have to do with goals and work and seeking out what you want in life and going after it. That's because, if you haven't guessed it by now, I have a bit of an obsessive personality. When I set my mind on doing something, you can almost always consider it done. And there is nothing I am more obsessed with than paths. You see, in the literal sense, I've been digging them around foundations for most of my life. And as you already know, I've also helped hundreds of my employees forge their own paths in life while they were digging for my company. And just how do I spend my *free time* or my *time off of work*? You guessed it. I spend it on paths! All kinds of paths, trails, back roads, even golf courses (they are, after all, one long set of paths). Why do I spend my free time on paths? Because nothing gives me more clarity, more hope, or more inspiration than walking a path that I know will lead me to something wonderful.

I'd now like to explore our current understanding of the word *path*, which has many different dictionary definitions—so many, in fact, that I thought it important that we explore them right off the bat. *Path* can mean:

---

[*] *Stephen R. Covey,* The 7 Habits of Highly Effective People *(New York: Free Press, 1989).*

- A track that is especially made for people to walk on or ride on. A route or a course made for a particular purpose.
- A route or course along which someone or something travels or moves.
- A trail or route between one place or another.
- A set of actions that lead to a result or a goal.
- A narrow walk, or a way to somewhere.
- A path is a previously made walkway, usually clearly defined, with a beginning and an end, containing a measurable distance.
- A path leads, usually, **to a desired place**, thing, or result (and in many instances, in a predictable amount of time).

Paths. Based on any one of these definitions, we're on a path whether we know it or not. Right now you are walking on either a proverbial or a literal path, or both. But is your path taking you to *a desired place, goal, or result*? Is every step you take getting you closer to where you want to go, or further away?

Now I want you to think back to the last time you were actually on a path. Was it a well-worn walkway leading you to a favorite place to jog? Was it a trail in the woods leading you to a riverbank? Or maybe it was a cart path between golf holes? Do you remember how you felt when you first saw the path, when you first walked its winding curves? Think back until you arrive at a clear memory of it. Perhaps it's been a while since you have experienced it, but maybe it's high time you should again, because that feeling I'm describing of taking a long walk along a path that leads to a terminus—some sort of desired location, perhaps one with a breathtaking view of the ocean or a sweeping landscape filled with mountains and lush trees—isn't just a desired end. *It's the desired feeling you've been longing for,* but maybe, just maybe, you didn't realize it until right now. In other words, many of us don't know what's possible, what freedom and fun actually feels or looks like, because we're stuck walking in circles or we are busy jumping from one path to another, quitting and turning back before we get to reap the rewards of the glorious summit, spectacular view, or quiet meadow. Because we don't know how amazing things could be for us, we don't even try. Instead, we watch others live their seemingly incredible lives and then say things like:

- "Lucky gal, she has all the fun!"
- "Must be nice for you, dude."
- "Yeah, right, that's not in the cards for me."
- "Maybe someday, if I win the lottery."

We use all sorts of negative and self-limiting words. We cut ourselves off from the path to freedom before we even start because we have no idea how great it would feel if we did have the thing we always dreamed about, or if we did set some goals and follow the path. If we knew for one second how amazing and possible all of this could be, we would all be setting and crushing goals every day. Truth is, most of us are scared. We were told when we were young: *That's a dumb idea.* Or, *Why do you want to do that?* Or, *Maybe you should live your life this way because that's how I always did it.* Whenever we do what someone else expects, we aren't operating out of a sense of freedom or choice. We're not taking deliberate actions at all, or as Dr. Stephen Covey would say, we're allowing other people or circumstances to shape us and our lives.

What if I told you that feeling—that amazing feeling you get from accomplishing something—could be yours? Would you pick a path and follow it? Let's just put it this way, if Ken Rusk, once a scrappy, skinny kid with a facial deformity and no college education, can end up owning his own company, creating wealth, and traveling the world, then you can do it too. Anyone can.

FOLLOWING A PATH

Beginning when I was about five years old, my four brothers and I would spend almost every waking moment in the woods near our home. We did everything boys could possibly do when left to their own devices. We rode our banana bikes, chased one another through the creeks, shot BB guns, and sometimes just walked aimlessly. By midsummer, we would have well-worn trails that wound through the rolling valleys of our hometown neighborhood in the aptly named Sagamore Hills. It seemed there was always a gas line, electric line utility, or oil exploration path that we would follow until it ended, or until we were so far away from home that even at that young age, we realized we'd better turn back. Sunup to sundown, we were in those woods. To us, a good long path was a symbol of daring, risk, and most important, relief, as it would invariably lead us back home. It seemed to us that those paths were a place of risk, yet safety—the safety of knowledge and discovery—a lifeline in a world that had yet to see cell phones or GPS devices. Yep, a good path was the best kind of road map you could ask for. Strange as it may sound, you could always trust them. We always ended up somewhere pretty cool. Guaranteed.

The years went by, and life happened. My brothers and I got cars, jobs, and girlfriends, and we really didn't have as much use for those hills and the trails we cut through them. And yet from that point on, it seemed that any time I happened upon a new path, I would feel a sense of comfort, a calming peace, and a *palpable freedom*. Those paths were part of my fabric, and I knew it. The feeling was unmistakable.

And so whenever I discover an interesting path for the first time, I always wonder how it was made. I think about the very first time someone walked it, and how this particular spot was so interesting, so intriguing, that many people were called to follow it, over and over until the earth was beautifully trampled into a long, narrow, timeless work of art.

It wasn't until the fall of 2000, when I was visiting Scotland for the first time, that I came to know just how important the concept of *the paths* taken through life would be to me. It was then when I first came to realize that I needed to use my experiences to try to help others obtain the freedom that I had. (Ultimately, this idea would manifest itself in helping me shape many parts of this book.)

Allow me to back up a bit. I'm an amateur golfer. I really, really like the game . . . *a lot*. As far as I am concerned, it's the greatest game ever invented. For me, there is an overwhelming sense of serenity on a golf course. It's what I love to do in what's called my "free time." When it's just me, the course, my choice of club, and 6,800 yards of the most beautiful scenery imaginable, I am self-reliant. Whatever happens, I'm in charge of my own fun. The beautiful thing about singular sports like golf is that everything is on you—the good, bad, or mediocre. I may not be in charge of the circumstances or the course conditions, but I can pretty much count on what *I* bring to the course. And that's an awesome feeling.

Over the years, it's also been a source of goal-setting for me. I can always improve something—my swing, the way I hold the club, or how I putt. There are other things that I can set goals around—like *where* I play.

Back in the early nineties, my buddies and I came up with the idea of planning a trip to the home of golf: the Old Course in St. Andrews, Scotland, considered the oldest golf course in the world. It was a huge goal—and by huge, I mean seemingly impossible for me and my sixteen friends. It was the Mac Daddy of all golf trips. This was not our typical Northern Michigan weekend warrior trip that we were planning. This time we would be filing for passports, booking several hotel rooms thousands of miles away, arranging airfare through multiple time zones, packing large suitcases, shipping precious golf clubs, and making arrangements for all the other scary traveler stuff, like buying travelers insurance. This would require some serious planning—oh, and lots of dough, a lot more than we were used to spending or most of us had ever dreamed of spending on a trip for ourselves (without spouses or family members). This was huge for us.

And so the planning began. Remember, this was a bucket-list event. We decided to go big or go home. When else in our lives would we be able to take a trip like this?

We decided to create a "dream" itinerary and worry about the costs later. We asked ourselves: *What do we really want to do? What would a dream vacation look like?* We all agreed it would be absolutely epic. We wanted to play as many courses as possible. That would mean crisscrossing Scotland to play all the world-famous courses—not only the Old Course, but also Carnoustie, Western Gailes, Kingsbarns, and Turnberry. Our schedule would require our own custom travel bus, a driver, and a porter. We also wanted to stay in historic castles turned into bed-and-breakfasts. *Why not go authentic?* And soon a dream golf trip was laid out on paper for all of us to see. Now to rip off the Band-Aid and look at the damage: How much was this going to cost us?

My friend Steve, who had some experience with these things, ran the numbers and delivered the bad news. It turned out that our "epic" excursion was going to set each of us back . . . nearly *five thousand dollars*! As we leaned back in our chairs, we scratched our heads and tried hard not to let this dream die right then and there. That's when a lightbulb went off. I said, "We shouldn't allow this trip to be an IF. . . . It just needs to become a WHEN." As some of them looked at me puzzled, I went on to say that if we just pushed the date off far enough, each of us could save enough money to get the job done and make this once-in-a-lifetime experience really happen.

After some simple math on a restaurant napkin, we made a decision. We would plan the trip for **three years from that meeting**. Why three years? Simple—you already know why. We broke it down into manageable parts. We decided that we could all save about thirty bucks a week, put it aside in separate bank accounts, and let it build for 156 weeks. Sounds crazy, but we knew that those years would fly by in anticipation of our trip. And it was at that precise moment that we knew our Scotland adventure would become a reality. . . . The dream golf trip changed from a someday to a today, instantly changing from an IF to a WHEN.

There is a tidal wave of cool feelings once an amazing path

plan is set in motion. The great feelings beget great feelings, and those feelings were there long before the wheels ever went up on the plane. We were experiencing "freedom"—through deliberate action, long before we experienced our "free time" in Scotland.

Later, I would think a lot about the impact that simple golf trip calculation would have on the way I lived my life. I had imagined a path, a clearly defined trail with a beginning and an end, a route between that restaurant table and golf's birthplace, a walkway that had 156 weekly stepping-stones to it, each representing $30 and a set of actions that would almost certainly lead to our desired result. We had a measurable amount of time needed to complete it. I had put my own goal path in motion, and it had worked!

The reality is that just like those good feelings, freedom begets freedom. When you start making deliberate choices for yourself and how you use your time, before you know it you are doing things that make you feel freer, more self-reliant, and more alive. Your ultimate path to freedom requires that you acknowledge the preciousness of your time. After taking stock of what you're doing, you can then start focusing on what you want. And how do you know what you do want? You'll know by the desired feeling: The *oh man, I can't believe this* kind of feeling. I still remember turning to my buddy when we touched down in Scotland and saying pretty much the same thing: "Can you believe we're actually doing this?"

That is freedom, man. There is incredible freedom in living a life you're in charge of, doing things that make you feel comfortable, peaceful, and free. It doesn't matter what you do for a living, or where you go (or don't go) to school—you can be free. You already have everything you need inside of you.

And you also have time. As short as we determined our time is on earth, the amount of time in a day is the same for everyone on the planet. We're all operating with the same twenty-four. And *you* get to decide what *you* do with that time. You get to decide what desired feelings and experiences you want to have. You get to choose your ultimate path to freedom. You can go on world-class vacations, you can buy the car you want, you can do whatever it is you want to do with your "free time" once you put the goal path in action. Don't let anyone tell you that because of what you do for a living you won't have access to the feelings of comfort, peace, and freedom. Once you decide how you are going to spend your precious time and resources in life, your entire world is going to open up. You'll be free from worrying about what others think. (You don't have time for that!) You'll be free from all the drama and negativity in life. (You have better places to go and people to hang out with! Time's a-wasting!) And every step that you take *away* from the feelings and experiences you *don't* want, you're moving *toward* the places and desired feelings you *do* want. That's awesome. That's freedom.

So dig in. Take an inventory of your time spent. Set a timer for twenty-four hours and let it run, noting what you're doing in a journal or notebook at intervals throughout the day. How are you spending your time? Are you spending it on the things that are moving you closer or further away from freedom? Are you self-reliant and self-determined? Do you set yourself on paths, or are you waiting for someone to give you permission? What is your "Scotland"? Is there something you want to experience before your Life Clock runs out? Can you put a goal path in place to help you make sure it comes true? I've put together a list of steps you can follow to take your dreams from raw vision to successful completion. The following is a "how-to" set of actions you can take to becoming who YOU want to be and finally starting your new comfortable, peaceful, and freedom-filled life.

FIVE STEPS TO ACHIEVING ANY GOAL

While coaching dozens of people in my organization on how to obtain just about any goal, I have experimented with many different methods, and have settled on just five steps that anyone can follow. The first thing you'll see is that they are quite simple. That's by design. The simpler they are, the more likely you will follow them. So let's take a look at the five steps together.

STEP 1: WELL DONE!

This is the easiest step of all. All you have to do is *congratulate yourself.* Say it out loud. WELL DONE! You heard me right. Congratulate yourself for getting off the couch of procrastination and beginning the process of bettering yourself. Seriously, do it! Use a mirror if you have to. Why am I so insistent here? The answer is this: You have just separated yourself from the majority of people who roam this earth waiting for things to "get better," or, better stated, waiting for life to happen *to them* instead of them happening *to life.* We as human beings have an innate ability to just "be" and to accept the status quo. We sell ourselves on the idea that we are *just fine.* We tell ourselves to stay the way we are. No need to risk putting ourselves out there to make our life better; it's all good just the way it is. So we stay on that couch. After all, it is comfortable there, right?

Wrong.

Remember the Virginia Tech study I briefly mentioned in the first chapter, the one about how few people even pay attention to their life goals? The study is cited in Dan Zadra's bestselling, inspirational *The 5 Book: Where Will You Be Five Years From Today?** The study used one hundred subjects to carefully observe the human capacity for setting and achieving goals. Zadra reports that 80 percent of us admit to not having any goals whatsoever. That means most of us are not dreaming about our futures at all! As a person who repeatedly sets and achieves goals, I find this shocking. The study goes on to say that only 16 percent of us admit to having goals, but even this 16 percent don't bother to memorialize them or document them in any way. I would call these *dreamers*, plain and simple—*lifetime members of the Somedayers Club*, a term I'll explain in the next chapter.

As if that was not surprising enough, Zadra reports that only a minuscule 4 percent of us actually write down our goals, and only one out of those four people who actually take out a pen and paper, only one—YES JUST ONE—single respondent actually took the critical step of keeping their written goal *out in front of them* and reviewed their progress on a regular basis. The other three, however resolute they are in their convictions, will still just stick the goal list in the kitchen drawer and likely never think of it again (until, perhaps, they come across it while looking for a bottle opener for that beer they'll be guzzling while zoning out in front of the television). It should be no secret that the rarefied group—the 1 percent who takes their

* *Dan Zadra, The 5 Book: Where Will You Be Five Years from Today? (Seattle: Compendium, Incorporated, Publishing & Communications, 2009).*

goal-setting most seriously—ends up hitting most if not all of the goals they aspire to achieve.

And let's not forget the key takeaway here: *That 1 percent earns eight times more income over their lifetimes than the rest of the bunch!* Goals . . . pretty powerful stuff—am I right?

I'd now like you to write down these statistics and sit back and look at them. C'mon now, put this book down, go get a pen and a piece of paper, and write these numbers down:

- 80 percent of us have no goals at all.
- 16 percent have goals but don't document them in any way.
- 4 percent write down their goals.
- 1 percent pay attention to their written goals.
- That same 1 percent earns eight times more income than the other 99 percent.

Okay, now take a good long look at them. Ask yourself which category you currently fall into. Let's think about your potential to change. Now ask yourself these questions:

- *Which of these groups AM I a part of?*
- *Which of these groups WOULD I be a part of?*
- *Which of these groups COULD I be a part of?*
- *Which of these groups SHOULD I be a part of?*

Now I want you to congratulate yourself for starting this process of setting a goal. Just by doing this one thing, you are joining 16 percent of the population—a rare group, indeed. But don't stop there. Make a promise to yourself right now, right here, that whatever goal you set out to do, you will write it down. You will keep it somewhere you can see it, and you will give yourself the recognition you deserve for going down a path toward ultimate achievement that only 1 percent of the population has the drive to travel.

STEP 2: IDENTIFY THE GOAL

We have discussed at length the importance of being able to visualize, in vivid detail, as many parts of the life you want as possible. Remember the crayon drawing from chapter one? It's time to take that artwork apart, piece by piece, vision by vision, goal by goal.

First let's pick the easiest ones, the "low-hanging fruit," if you will. Find a goal you *know* you can achieve in a few months or less. It could be to finally pay off a nagging bill, or a reasonable weight loss, or the purchase of a new big-screen TV. It could be something like achieving a milestone at work, or increasing your pay, or adding one or two new clients. Or it could be, since this book is about building a life without a college degree, finding a lucrative, blue-collar job or a career that you desire, that you can see yourself doing, and at which you are confident you can make a living.

No matter what goal you choose, it should be something that will have a forwarding impact and stir a positive emotion in you. Choose something that will make you proud, something that will relieve some stress. Remember that five-gallon bucket we talked about? What emotions are brimming to the surface right now? What negative emotions would you like to replace? If you're anxious about bills, let's replace that stressed-out and anxious emotion with a positive one that is backed with a positive action: *"I am going to pay off that pesky credit card bill and be done with it once and for all. I am going to do it. And I am never going to think of it again."*

Ah, how does that feel? You can do it. *You can do anything.* You're not a powerless victim of stress and anxiety. You have some choices—and you can take some positive steps now.

Remember, each one of these mini wins is for the purpose of creating comfort, peace, and freedom in your life. Each successful path to completion will make you feel that much more confident in your ability to set and achieve goals in the future. Small victories beget larger ones. Your confidence will grow as you begin to see how much control you actually have over who you are and who you ultimately want to be. So start by focusing now on just one small, attainable goal.

Got it? Good. It's now time for us to dive a bit deeper in breaking down the goal, to lay the final stepping-stones on our path to comfort, peace, and freedom.

STEP 3: BUILD CERTAINTY

This is the most challenging step toward a solid, successful path design. It takes some careful, honest planning.

The key is to build in the certainty that you will, in fact, succeed. Remember, it's not the time it takes to get to your stated goal that is so important, but the fact that you are SURE to get there. That is why being honest with yourself is so critical here. You will be chopping your goal into many small pieces, or stepping-stones, that will make up your path. Each piece will be something you can accomplish week in and week out *with certainty,* so be careful *and be real* with yourself when determining the amount of energy, attention, or cash you are willing to commit.

Believe me, this is where success or failure happens. Don't

get hung up on the number of pieces, or steps, you build in the process. Just focus on taking one step at a time. Again, it will never matter how long the path is, just that you have designed it correctly. Breaking apart goals into meaningful, actionable, measurable steps is the best way to achieve them. The path must have a beginning and an end, with a clear number of steps carefully laid out by you, and no way to get off or turn back once you have started walking.

Let's take a real example. Say you want to lose fifty pounds. Don't try to do it in a couple of months. Set a reasonable goal and then break down the goal. Plan on losing one pound a week for fifty weeks. It's said that one pound is equivalent to 3,500 calories. Okay, so that means you have to *reduce* 3,500 calories or *burn* 3,500 calories in a week. What does that mean for your goal path? It means reducing your calories by just five hundred calories a day. Is that so difficult? It's equivalent to two snacks or two glasses of wine, or some simple form of exercise that will burn the five hundred calories. (Or you can do some combination of the two—running for half an hour and eliminating one snack.) Your ultimate goal is to lose fifty pounds in fifty weeks. Your weekly goal is to lose one pound. Your daily goal is to cut back or burn five hundred calories. Your hourly goal is to make choices that support your ultimate goal.

See how this works? Once you make the choice, you know what you need to do to achieve your goal, and then you simply execute. Day by day, week by week, and before you know it, fifty weeks will vaporize in front of you. You'll not only be fifty pounds lighter, you'll be exponentially healthier too. You'll probably be feeling more energized and active and more willing to take on other goals.

This is just an example, but you see what I mean. If weight

isn't an issue, try tackling a small bill. Recently an employee who has been with our company for several years approached me. She had been watching others use the path design process and decided to participate. She wanted to think BIG, yet she was worried about committing to her path. She had family in Europe whom she had never met, and it was her goal to visit them. "If only *someday* I could get over there to see them," she said to me. Like so many of us, it was a goal she thought was too lofty, and she was worried about getting her hopes up and ultimately being disappointed in herself. Fear was her biggest obstacle—fear of failing, fear of being disappointed. Well, that fear wasn't going to get her on a plane to Europe! I knew she had to—and *could*—do something about this. I knew this was a BIG GOAL, but it wasn't an impossible one. So she and I set about making it a reality.

The first thing we did was figure out the price for the entire trip. Soon she had the amount she could commit to set aside to make this family reunion a reality. A few minutes later, the path was designed. The entire trip would cost $2,200. She had already slowly, but sporadically, accumulated a few hundred dollars toward this endeavor. But then, just by saving $30 a week for sixty-three weeks, she was able to see her family in Europe the very next spring. I was overjoyed to see the excitement on her face as she called her sister to share the news that she was going to Europe. All of this was made possible simply because she decided to remove herself from the sidelines and get in the game. To paraphrase a line from the classic film *The Shawshank Redemption*, she got busy living instead of busy dying. Once she committed to a path, nothing could hold her back.

This method can be used to achieve any goal you can imagine. So what are you waiting for? Let's get out your Crayola drawing. Pick one area of your vision and then decide to make it a goal. Determine your level of certainty to handle each step. Figure out your completion date. Plan how you will achieve each milestone. Then LAUNCH. You are now ready to take step four.

STEP 4: SET IT, DON'T SWEAT IT

Part of the beauty of designing path plans and designing your life in this way is the "set it, don't sweat it" process by which we accomplish our goals. Keep in mind this is meant to be an automatic process, one that happens week in and week out, with or without your constant awareness. The goal is to make your goals effortless. Are you with me?

So, how is this done? This fourth step is where the machine gets turned on and we watch it work. But first, let's quickly review what we've done thus far, shall we?

In step one, you congratulated yourself for getting off the procrastination couch.

In step two, you identified a target you just HAVE to hit.

In step three, you've designed the stepping-stones with certainty along the path to your success. (Goal = small steps x increments of time.)

Now we put the plan into action. *Step four is all about the walk.* This is where you physically sign up for that class and commit to its completion. This is where you join that gym and set up your workout routine with the trainer—days, times, calories in, calories out, pounds lost, everything. This is where you go to your payroll office with a blank check in hand and set up an automatic deposit of your wages into a savings account that you purposefully restrict your own access to, even in emergencies.

Do I make myself clear? You will hit your goal, come hell or high water, and the best part is, it will be done automatically.

You are putting things in motion. You have a "do or die" and "no going back" mentality. You are walking this path. You can see the end from the beginning. You are on your way. You own this now, you believe in it fully, and your confidence is starting to spike. You are living in the world of anticipation, the best world of all. Feelings of accomplishment are already beginning to seep into your fifth gallon, and it feels great! You are in control of your own life and your own vision or version of comfort, peace, and freedom. Congratulations again. You are now in a club that only one out of a hundred people join!

STEP 5: TIME TO SHARE

At this point, we need to talk about creating an insurance policy that will guarantee that you won't back down or step off the path. We need to create a solid defense against life's unexpected obstacles—the minor pitfalls and daily distractions—yes, all those little monsters that try to get us off our well-designed path. You know what I am talking about—all the things that try to force us to lose our mojo, stop walking the path, or worse, force us to turn around and go back. Our minds are amazing machines. They can support us in the strength of our stick-to-it-iveness, or they can sabotage us and attempt to justify the failures, even try to scare us into abandoning the path altogether.

The good news is that we can avoid this wayward action by counting on the strength of others. That old adage "there is power in numbers" still holds true, and it is at the very heart of our next and final step in bulletproof path-planning. All you have to do is find someone who cares about you and who believes in you and your potential, and then share your goals with that person or those persons. Have you ever heard the saying, "Two heads are better than one"? Spoiler alert: it's true.

Let's take this a step further. Find someone to get involved in your goal. (You'll find them in the *Todayers Club*, which I'll discuss in the next chapter.) Choose wisely. You want to choose someone who encourages you, supports you, wants to see you succeed. You also want someone who has his or her own goals. Once you identify this person, don't just *tell* them about it, SHARE it with them. Let me explain the important distinction between these two words. "Telling" is easy. Simply point your face toward another person and begin speaking. But "sharing" is another story. In fact, it is a concept I believe should be defined, so here I go.

To share means to be part of something bigger. We share space on this planet with about six billion other people. We share responsibilities—at work, at home, in our community. In other contexts, we also own *shares*—we own parts of companies through stocks and bonds. We take a part of a whole. We benefit constantly from a "shared" economy. We give, we take, we buy, we sell. And when we engage in the *activity* of sharing, we are often telling someone about something, usually something personal about ourselves. When we *share* in doing something, we each play a designated role. We each *participate*. When you are setting a goal, you want to be sure you have someone with whom *to share* your accomplishments and achievements. You want someone who will walk the walk with you. You want them to be as committed to your success as you are. They will need to accept that you have changed the way you think, the way you see your future, and how you plan to get there. You will be thinking bigger than they might be used to as well. Your new path partner should feel honored that you have entrusted them with something so profoundly meaningful to you.

Path partners will bring a multitude of benefits to the path walker and nearly always help to ensure success. Your mind will kick into an entirely new gear once you have publicly stated your desire to another. Many times, your own belief in what you are about to do will increase, as will your confidence in its execution. Your path partner will be there to check in on your progress, walk the path with you, pick you up if you stumble, encourage you when you need it, and strengthen your resolve.

In my own life, when I think of my best example of sharing a goal, my thoughts hearken back to my childhood, to an experience I'm sure I share with many others. Remember the first time you and your friends stared up at the high dive? Okay, maybe not the thirty-foot high dive, maybe the middle one below that. I am sure it was still daunting the first time you considered jumping off of it. I am willing to bet that before you found the courage and commitment to take that first jump, you probably spent an hour or so talking to your friends about it. I am sure they egged you on. Am I right? Now here is the important part. Tell me how you felt once the negotiation was over and you had to walk to the ladder and start climbing those paint-faded metal stairs. From the time your foot hit that first rung, to the point where you reached the board, how many times did you look over at your friends, who were anxiously watching your every move? I'm going to guess it was many times. I can imagine you nervously checking the resolve on their faces, while they checked the resolve on yours. But you weren't done yet, were you? You walked slowly down the board, and as you neared the end, you began to feel the board give under your weight, almost warning you to go back. You gave another check of your friends' faces down below. As they stared back at you, their expressions ranged from disbelief to outright fear. You soon realized that if you were ever going to do this, you had to release the white-knuckle grip you had on the side rails.

And there you were, precariously perched on the edge some fifteen feet in the air, about to take your three-second introduction into human flight. But what happened next says it all—*and is the essence of step five*. You see, as you stood there, wondering just how hard the water is at twenty-five miles per hour, you may have begun to waver a bit, to question the sanity of this entire endeavor. After all, your life was just fine before you decided to climb these stairs and launch your sixty-seven-pound body off a fiberglass cliff, right? And so you looked for reassurance one more time. When you needed it the most, you looked down at your friends, your path partners, and you saw what you were hoping for—what you were counting on all along. Yes, there in the faces of those you trust, you saw smiles, nods of encouragement, and fist pumps, and you heard "You can do it!" This was incredibly powerful stuff. It emboldened you. It gave you courage. So what did you do? You turned back to the board and faced your fears, moved forward a bit, swallowed that lump in your throat, and . . . LAUNCHED!

So, the question becomes, how much of a role did your aquatic companions play in the success of your dive? I am guessing at least 50 percent, at a minimum. The power of sharing your goal plans with supportive path partners simply cannot be overestimated. There is power in knowing that you have the good wishes and positive vibes, even the daily prayers, of others who walk the path along with you, hand on your shoulder, keeping you steady at times as you move on down the line.

PITFALLS TO AVOID

Just as the boy on the diving board had enthusiastic, supportive friends to help him accomplish his goal, the opposite can be true as well. This is why it is SO important to choose wisely when it comes to those who you rely on to offer help when you need it.

Let's go back to the story of Natalia the YouTube influencer. Part of her journey to success contained a dark period in her life when she nearly lost everything . . . all because she chose to share her journey with the wrong "friends." It turns out that while she was amassing millions of hits, views, and followers of her YouTube video content, Natalia decided to move to California to be closer to her industry, enjoy her success, and live in the world of the *influencers*.

Soon Natalia was sharing an apartment with other successful entrepreneurs, and it wasn't very long before the "good life" got out of hand. Her "friends" who she shared her goals and work life with were not only unsupportive but ended up nearly destroying her and her career. It seems the line between who she really was and the person she created online began to blur. All-night parties and drug and alcohol abuse were encouraged and rampant. Natalia was spiraling out of control, and her so-called support system did nothing to help her, especially since their own lives were plunging into chaos as well. Telling me her story, she held back tears as she described how her mother would try to contact her to help, but eventually gave up. Cut off from communication with her daughter, she saw her only on her YouTube channel. Natalia went on to tell me that her mother constantly cried as she watched her own daughter slowly deteriorate week in and week out from the constant drug use. Natalia felt shame and sadness for having put her mother through that. You could say that the one person who wanted to champion her the most was sent to the sidelines, while the wrong crowd stepped in and took her place.

This is a lesson in sharing. When you choose to take the critical (and life-changing) step of setting a goal that is really important to you, you are, in a sense, going to put yourself out on a limb. I have often said that if I have a workout partner waiting for me at the gym each morning, I will have a much better chance of achieving my desired result than if I try to go it alone. Having that right someone to be there for you, to guide you, to help you, to steady you, and to put a hand on your shoulder when you need it (and you will need it) is one of the most crucial things you can do to ensure your success.

SUMMARY OF THE FIVE-STEP METHOD

If you want to achieve peace in life, you have to be willing to be present. You have to be engaged with the life you have in front of you. You have to be willing to do something every day that will alleviate stress and anxiety—not create more of it.

The best way I know how to achieve peace in life is to have clearly defined goals in all areas of your life. Goals give us something to work on daily. You can achieve these goals by following five steps:

- First, you congratulated yourself for being someone who is goal-oriented and goal-driven.
- Second, you identified the goal you want to achieve. Why is this goal so important to you?
- Third, you built in the steps you know you *can* achieve. You reviewed your Crayola-crayon-designed life and picked one part of the picture and are determined to work on it. You broke down the steps you need to make this goal a reality. How much are you willing to commit to it each week? How many hours, dollars, how much energy, etc.? Given these amounts, how long will it take you to reach your goal?
- Fourth, you launched. You did something every single day toward your goal, and you're not sweating the outcome. You already know you're going to achieve it. You also know *when* you are going to achieve it because *you built that into the process*!
- And fifth, you found someone along the way to share your achievements (and struggles) with you. What plans do you have in place to communicate with them regularly?

I've seen hundreds of people who, by following these simple steps, have achieved the goals they had previously only talked and dreamed about, so I know it can be done. And I know you have it in yourself to achieve anything you put your mind to. If you want to live a peaceful life, goal-setting is a great place to start. So dig in.

9

GOING IT ALONE, READY FOR LAUNCH: A STORY OF PERSISTENCE AND RESILIENCE

Building your own business can be a goal for every craftsman. You might call it the American dream, and you'd be right. Each year, millions of energetic, enthusiastic men and women take a shot at working for themselves, being their own boss, controlling their own destiny, and hopefully making a profit. I did it myself, and many times I look back on the path that got me here and think, *There is no better way to live.* I wouldn't have changed a thing. Getting the chance to work with my hands in construction all these years has treated me well. Yes, the blue-collar industry is one of the very best places to start a business you can call your very own, do what you love, admire what you've created, and make a great living doing it.

And so I thought I would dedicate this chapter to the ingredients I believe are necessary to launch a successful endeavor. I would like to get beyond the typical attributes that accomplished business owners possess. You know, things like honesty, integrity, fairness, trust, doing what you say and doing it on time. Mind you, those many qualities are vital to creating an enterprise you can be proud of. I have known many successful business owners, and I get asked all the time what I think are the keys to their longevity in the business world.

Now, let's just say for a moment that you are not particularly interested in running your own company. Read on anyway, because what I am about to share with you can be used in any part of your life. I'll share with you three concepts that I believe are the foundation of anyone wishing to make a change in their life, whether it is creating your own business, or deciding to make a major career move. I'll share these three ideas, plus a couple of stories to illustrate their meanings.

I'VE NEVER BUILT A SKYSCRAPER

Most of us have never started our own company. It's a daunting task, ripe with the risk of leaving our comfort-zone easy chair on which we've been sitting for a very long time. We'd be leaving our cushy, if not financially sound, past behind. And then there is the humility of losing our life savings should the process not go so well. Yes, it is easy to just do nothing, risk nothing, learn nothing, and become less than your potential. But before you think you don't have the right stuff, allow me to help you set your mind in the right place.

Many years ago, I heard (though I have long forgotten

the source) the most inspiring yet simple life lesson that can help anyone do just about anything. It is a lesson I have shared countless times over the last thirty-two years, during hundreds of sales meetings, staff meetings, and one-on-one personal goal sessions. I call it the How to Build a Skyscraper. And it is a valuable learning tool I hope you enjoy.

For the purposes of this story, let's use a skyscraper as our example. I wanted to use something complex, difficult to get your head around, and certainly something you've never imagined doing.

Now then, I want you to say this out loud: *I've never built a skyscraper, but if I did, I would probably* ....

The reason why this is an important step is because it forces you to take on the task as if you *have* done it before. This is very different from knowing the end of the path. Acting as if you know what you're doing will give you the added confidence not only to build an amazing building but also to tackle any project or problem in life.

So let's take this a bit deeper. You see, no matter how difficult, complex, or seemingly impossible a goal or task might appear at first, you can accomplish it if you have the desire to dig in—if you're willing to imagine the process as if you've already done it, and if you're willing to learn all that you don't yet know. I want to reiterate this fact. You can do anything *when you're willing.* You can do anything if you *feel* like you've done it before.

This can bring you an enormous sense of calm as you think about starting your own business. So much of our anxiety comes from fear—fear that we can't do something, fear that others are judging us, and the most popular of all fears, fear that we will fail. Let me tell you something: there is enormous power and peace in knowing that no matter what comes up in life, you have the capacity within you to handle it. Need proof? Look no further than *the world around you*. If humans have been able to make this earth, which is basically a spinning ball of rock, soil, air, and water, into everything you see, hear, smell, taste, and touch, then yes, even you can build a skyscraper—and just about anything else you can imagine. How? Simple: you just work your way backward.

WORKING YOUR WAY BACKWARD

Whether you're constructing a huge building, thinking about opening your own hair salon, deciding to learn a trade, or facing a serious problem at home, you need to stop and look at what you hope the end result will be. Before you take the first step, I want you to think about where you *want to end up*. I want you to think about the results you hope to achieve. Take in the entire "skyscraper," if you will. It's massive, right? But you've done this before. Seemingly impossible to wrap your brain around? Just thinking about all the materials and supplies that will be needed is daunting. *But it's fine, because you already see it. You see the whole building.*

And so it begins. You're already on your way. Now, let's say it again, out loud. "I've never built a skyscraper before, but if I did, I'd probably need a design vision, then I'd need a site." Do you see how this works? By making assessments and asking questions before acting, you've already started to problem solve. You're thinking through every step before you begin.

Next you ask yourself, "What else am I going to need? I am going to need skilled workers, materials, and, oh, wait, hold up, a design team. Someone is going to have to design the sky-scraper, right? An architect? Yes, that's where I'll start . . . with an architect."

Then you start thinking, *Okay, so if it needs to be designed, there should be some experts I need to call in to help too. I'll need someone who knows about engineering, someone who knows about construction, someone who knows about budgets. Oh, and I am probably going to need a supplier who can get the building materials I'll need. A steel supplier? An electrical supplier? A foundation company. Some HVAC systems?* And on and on it goes until you realize you are actually doing it! The more questions you ask yourself, the more answers come to light.

See where I am going with this? You went from being someone who had no idea how to build a doghouse, much less a tall building, to getting on the phone with a large project manager. You don't have to be an expert in any field to ask questions or to find other people who can help you. *You don't have to have all the answers.* You need to find the people who do have the answers. You can take any problem apart, assess what you need at each step, and then follow the right course of action. By keeping the endgame in mind, in this case the vision of the building itself, you are almost forced to progress through the project. That's because the mind is constantly breaking down the project into smaller and smaller tasks, each one appearing to be less and less insurmountable until they become easier and easier to complete. Are you understanding the concept? It is quite simple to imagine, and very effective once deployed. But again, for it to be effective, you need to think in reverse, starting from the end and traveling to the beginning, and ask yourself the right questions, then find the people with the answers.

My first experience with applying this simple concept came

to me in the winter of 1983. I was just twenty years old and had been assigned the task of opening a franchised outpost of the company I was currently working for. The owner of our company was a hard-driving, shoot-first-and-ask-questions-later, details-be-damned kind of manager. "We are opening a franchise in Chicago," he said to me one day. "I need you to go out there and get it going." That's all I got. Simple as that. No instructions, no map, no owner's manual, nothing. And I mean *nothing.* We had no people, no prospects, no budget, no equipment, not even an office. What we DID have was an impossible deadline for opening, an artificial timeline my boss somehow invented in that skyscraper building head of his.

Off I went, silently chanting the "skyscraper" questions in my mind, hoping that the answers would just present themselves as I went along.

I spent the next month searching for locations with the novice owner of the new franchise. I remember he had just enough money to purchase franchise territory from us, but not quite enough experience. Actually, he had *no* experience. And so we kept at it, finally settling on a location—an office building, which was really just a shell of a building that I would have to figure out how to get finished. I met with a real estate agent (first time in my life), he hooked me up with a builder (first time in my life), I bought a phone system (first time in my life), I designed the space (first time in my life), and I yelled and screamed at Chicago's finest contractors (definitely the first time in my life). The contractors not only didn't listen to me or care what I was saying, but they also were a foot taller and 150 pounds heavier than I was.

"I've never built a franchise before, but if I did, I would probably _____," I repeated often.

It wasn't easy. Walls were built, finished, and painted. Offices were furnished, phones got up and running, a staff was hired, and off we went. We worked sunup to sundown making it happen, and ten weeks later, after one burst appendix (mine), the office was open for business.

I had built the skyscraper, just by asking myself one question at a time.

I share this life lesson with you for a simple reason. You can substitute the word *skyscraper* for nearly anything you can imagine!

> Just ask yourself this question:
> "I've never built a _____ before, but if I DID . . . then I probably
> would _____."

TO BUILD A SKYSCRAPER, YOU NEED COMMITMENT

Recently I had the honor of witnessing this very concept, not for the first or last time, in action. A friend of mine had an idea for a consumer app for everyday use. He wanted to create an app that would help people cart their large items home from Home Depot, Target, or any other big-box store if they didn't have a vehicle large enough to carry them.

For example, let's say you go to the store for a flowerpot. By the time you're finished shopping, you have a pot, six bags of topsoil, and a cool wooden arbor that was on sale. *You just couldn't pass it up, could you?* Problem: you drove the Ford Focus to the store, and now you have no way of getting all this great stuff home. Answer: touch an app on your phone, and in ten minutes a local guy and his pickup truck appear to cart your payload safely home. All for a small fee. It's like Uber for your newly purchased lawn mower or big-screen television. I was fascinated by my friend's concept, and honored he was asking for my help.

Granted, he had no specific training or experience in this field. He had no instructions on how to build such a company. He had never built this "skyscraper" before. What he did have was a great idea and a dump-truck load of ownership and commitment in pursuing it. He had shown me his ability to work hard to make this project a success. And that was all I needed to know to become an investor.

Besides working your way backward and breaking things down into simpler parts, you're going to need to have what my friend had: commitment and a willingness to work hard. You're going to need to persevere. Building your own "skyscraper" takes an enormous amount of stamina and determination. You have to pace yourself. But it's okay, because you've done this before! You have to forgive yourself for the errors you make along the way. You're not going to have all the right answers the first time. You're going to make mistakes, and you will learn from them and not make the same mistake a second time.

If you want to maintain peace in your life, you need to harness the confidence of building something you've never built before. That said, you also have to expect that things will not work out perfectly. You have to expect you're going to need to break things down into smaller and more doable actions. The good news is, when you stay present at the task at hand, when you do one thing at a time, when you keep your cool knowing it will all work out in the end, then I assure you, you will accomplish your objective, whatever it is—even if the project is as big as a skyscraper.

SOMETIMES THE PATH CAN BE PRETTY FOGGY

The plans are not always written out for you. Life doesn't come with an instruction manual, that's for sure, although there *are*, of course, some well-worn instruction manuals out there: go to school, get good grades, attend college, get a job, work your way up, and on and on and on. But many of us know those manuals don't always work for everyone, and they certainly don't always plan for "operator errors," "malfunctions," or the random "just go and do it." Most of what we do in life *does not* come with an instruction manual . . . like how to plan your future, how to make friends, how to maintain a healthy and long marriage, how to raise an infant into a good person and a contributing member of society, or how to navigate your way through the complex construction of your own self-built skyscraper. Every single one of us is going to build our own version of a skyscraper many times over in life. We're going to have to figure out how to do it on our own, and we're going to take different paths and different lengths of time to get where we are going. Whatever goals you have (and whatever obstacles you face along the way), I want you to know you have the ability to accomplish anything—all the while maintaining your peace. In fact, it's being done as we speak all over this great country.

Skyscrapers are being built every day. And just think about this for a moment—at some point in their careers, for every one of these builders it was their very first time!

Here's some specific pointers:

1. Think about these lessons as they relate to your own life. What is the "skyscraper" you want to build? What questions do you need to ask yourself to begin? Try this out: "I've never built a _____ before, but if I did, I would probably start by _____."
2. Assess your commitment to the project. How resilient are you, how persistent? Are you willing to do the work required to see it through to its completion? Can you see yourself in your rearview with the task accomplished?
3. If you have a "skyscraper" in mind but aren't ready to get started, what are you afraid of? What is holding you back? Are you worried you might fail? What steps can you put into action immediately to help alleviate your concerns?

RESILIENCE—THE ABILITY TO RECOVER FROM MISFORTUNE, DIFFICULTY, OR CHANGE

Another important attribute that is an absolute requirement for making a major career change and the happy life that goes with it is **resilience**. You're certainly going to need it if you decide to build your skyscraper.

What do I mean by *resilience*? I am talking about the ability to see things as they are and still be able to dig down deep inside yourself to say: *This too shall pass*, and more important, *I can bounce back from life's setbacks and roadblocks.* It means being positive and finding the silver lining in the darkest of circumstances. It means having perspective—seeing things in a different light. The most **resilient** people I know are able to say: *I can do things to help make my situation better.*

Let's be honest, life can be brutal. Some of us are born into horrific circumstances, while others of us get thrown some serious curveballs later in life that just flatten us right out. I can tell you, my daughter's melanoma certainly did that to me. **Resilience** is a way to help you during those times, and if you become adept at being **resilient**—before the curveball makes contact—it may in fact develop into a character trait that will guide you through whatever adversity, personal tragedy, suffering, loss, or unwanted permanent change might take place in your life.

Probably the most **resilient** person I know, someone who has had a tremendously positive impact on my life by his example, is my friend of more than twenty-seven years, Mark Martin. Mark is one of the happiest guys I know. He is an amazing family man, and a great friend to many, in addition to being the owner of a successful trucking and logistics company. Whether we're fishing, drinking, boating, or just hanging out, Mark makes every moment together memorable. He lives life to the fullest. So it would be easy for someone to look at Mark now and say: *What a lucky guy! He's really got it made!* Yet Mark's **resilience** and his unflappable character are things that were born out of necessity. He has been able to withstand tragedy, deal with it, heal from it, and somehow manage to come out whole on the other side. Mark is all this and then some, but his path to success was anything but *lucky.*

In 1978, when Mark was eighteen, he returned home from

school one day to find something out of a nightmare. Seeing his mother's car parked erratically in the garage and his step-father's truck concealed strangely in the rear of the house, Mark immediately sensed something was off. During his teen years, his stepfather had grown increasingly violent, and Mark was aware that his mom had been trying to end their fifteen-year marriage. Knowing his stepdad should not have been at the house at that time of day, Mark knew that something just wasn't right, that something bad, really bad, had happened. His gut wrenched, so instead of entering the house, he decided to call the police. When the officers entered his home, they dis-covered a gruesome scene. Mark's mother had been brutally murdered by his stepfather, who was eventually discovered in his idling truck in a barn behind the house, having committed suicide.

At just eighteen years old, Mark and his two brothers were alone. They had no one. Their biological father had left them years before, and now their mother had been murdered. To say Mark was devastated would obviously be an understatement. I can't imagine the unspeakable pain, grief, and shock he felt.

Needless to say, Mark spent the next year adrift. He calls this period in his life "mind-numbing." He could barely deal with the enormity of the tragedy when, barely out of his own childhood, he had to start handling family issues: settling the estate, selling the house, and dealing with all the other loose ends. On top of it, he had to support himself and his younger brother.

Not one to stay down for long, he had some adult decisions to make. Mark took a surprisingly high-pressure job at a box company. Standing at the end of a speeding conveyor belt and catching boxes, he was responsible for bundling them twenty-five at a time. During many thirty-minute lunch breaks, at the behest of his cranky supervisor, he had to spend time picking up boxes that had come too fast to bundle. However, the job did give him plenty of time to think. "This just can't be what I am supposed to do," he recalled saying to himself.

Back in his high school days, Mark had never spent much time thinking of higher education, but now the thought of the next chapter in his life led him to give it some consideration. Since his mother's death, he had spent a fair amount of time with lawyers and thought, *Maybe I'll be a lawyer . . . I can do what they do.* And so one day off he went to the University of Toledo. Feeling sure of himself, he walked into the registrar's office and asked to speak to someone who could register him for some law classes. When asked where he'd gone to "undergrad," he said: "I went to school in Oak Harbor."

The puzzled attendant questioned further. "Mr. Martin, I'm not aware of a college called Oak Harbor," to which Mark responded, "Oak Harbor High School. I did my undergrad at Oak Harbor High School!"

Mark has gotten a lot of traction with that funny, self-deprecating story over the years, and I think it points to one of his fundamental character traits. He's the type of person who thinks: *No limits.* He walked away from that exchange at the University of Toledo unabashed and undeterred. He knew he wanted and deserved a better life. He couldn't see himself catching boxes for the rest of his life, and he began a quest to figure out how to change his own destiny. Sure, law school would have been impossible without an undergraduate degree, so he reassessed his options and *bounced back.* **Resilience.**

Mark continued to work at the box company, but in the meantime, he married his longtime love, Cindy. He worked his

way up the line and became a machine manager. In no time
he was in charge of production, order fulfillment, and some
shipping and receiving. Over the next few years, he would
master all there was to know about that box fulfillment company, which made him a prime candidate to advance within
the organization. Soon he was managing people nearly twice
his age, improving production efficiencies, and cutting costs.
Ultimately, he moved to the company's headquarters in Michigan to try his hand at running the transportation department.

As his career progressed, so did his family, and soon Cindy
gave birth to their daughter, Amanda. Raising a family on one
salary was difficult, even though Mark was working sixty-hour
weeks in his new job, calculating shipping times and costs and
fulfilling orders for demanding customers. But he knew he
could do more, much more. Sure, as his responsibilities grew,
he received a few small raises here and there, but he felt there
was much more he was capable of doing. When it was time
for his annual review, he hoped for yet another well-deserved
increase in pay. Instead, his boss gave him the old "ceiling" conversation. "Mark," he told him, "you've already maxed out. You
are already earning what this job pays." When Mark pressed
him, reminding him of his accomplishments, his boss replied,
"Well, if you wanted more money, maybe you should have
become"—you guessed it—"a lawyer!"

For most people, this conversation would have been dis-
heartening, but not for Mark. He had what we call perspective.
He knew that there is bad news and then there is *my stepdad
killed my mom* bad news. Undeterred (another word for **resilient**), Mark left the office and had what he called an *aha* moment. He knew that his six years of experience, which included
twelve thousand hours of learning, doing, and then refining

this small business, would come in handy someday, and that gave him a drive that would fuel the rest of his career. And so when the next opportunity came to make an upwardly mobile change, he jumped at the chance. After a few years at his new job with a logistics company, Mark had come to the conclusion that it was poorly run by its owner. Mark knew the time had come to step out on his own, so on a Monday in early 1989, Cindy and Mark Transportation, aka Camway Transportation, was born.

Logistics, Mark has often told me, is all about relationships— relationships developed by good service. He had learned both sides of that equation—what *to* do, and more important, what *not* to do. The first day at Camway, Mark hit the ground running with eight sales calls. The company took off. He used the invaluable knowledge that came from his thousands of hours of grinding out a living to build a logistics company that began to ship items all over the world. During the next several years, he chartered hundreds of trucks, trains, ships, and aircraft to move his customers' freight on time and on target, with a huge emphasis on customer service. I remember being in his office in the early days, when he had a conference room table, much larger than most, covered with a few hundred impeccably organized truck tickets, each representing a particular delivery. It looked like an intensely busy war room a general might oversee, with navy men pushing little plastic battleships around a world map.

In 2004, a global trucking firm approached Mark to buy his company. After a few tough years of negotiating, a deal was done. Mark was just forty-three. He and Cindy could have sailed off into the sunset. In fact, they did that for a while, spending a few years boating in Florida, skiing in Colorado, and riding one of his many custom Harleys on Mark's annual trek to Sturgis, South Dakota.

But that's not where this story ends.

Up to this point, Mark had always led a positive, no-holds-barred, goal-driven life. He had boated all over South Florida, fished all he could fish, ridden his Harley Road King across the West to his heart's content, and skied to the mountains and back. And yet the goal that got him to this point remained. His drive endured.

And so, in early 2009 a new company, Cynamar Transportation, was born. Mark and Cindy were back in the game. Once again, the sound of trucks, planes, ships, and trains could be heard whistling through their newly built headquarters in Whitehouse, Ohio. The new company has grown every year, and I am certain it will meet whatever goals they have set.

At any point in time, Mark could have thrown up his arms and retired to live the good life. Hell, after what he had witnessed at eighteen years of age, who would have blamed him? But somewhere deep down he believed he deserved more, and that with hard work and a positive attitude, he could achieve anything he put his mind to. He never let "no" get in his way. He never let life's tragedies, disappointments, or even standing at the end of a conveyor belt, prevent him from the life he believed he deserved. And he did it all without going to law school, let alone any college at all.

How did he do it? Mark excelled at the task at hand. He learned on the job and applied those real-life lessons to his own life. Now, I know you can take classes in business school and even law school about customer relationships, but there is nothing that teaches the ins and outs of business like actually working and experiencing those relationships. True, Mark's story—a factory assembly line guy–turned–owner of a multimillion-dollar logistics company—is exceptional. But I absolutely know that it's not impossible. I've heard these stories my whole life. At eighteen years old, standing at the end of a conveyor belt and thinking to himself: *This isn't what I am supposed to do*, Mark put himself on a path of self-discovery. The moment you put rubber to the road, you can achieve what you desire. Mark Martin showed me that. I hope he shows you too, that no matter where you are right now in life, if you believe you deserve better and have a willingness to achieve better and are **resilient** like Mark, you will absolutely be able to accomplish anything you set yourself on the path to do.

PERSISTENCE—CONTINUING ON A COURSE OF ACTION IN SPITE OF DIFFICULTY

Just like **commitment** and **resilience**, persistence—the ability to keep going in the face of obstacles—is a cornerstone of any effective person or company. You are going to get knocked down, and you are going to encounter roadblocks along the way. You have to get back up, dust yourself off, and get back in the game. It is the only way you will ever break through. Here's the key, though: I am not describing just the business titans of the world, CEOs of major corporations and the like. Anyone can learn these three attributes. How can I say that? It's simple: if you feel strongly enough about an idea, the process, product, or service that you want to offer, those same attributes will grow inside you and become your DNA. You will be so passionate about the result, beginning with the end in mind, building your skyscraper, creating your successful business, that you will be unstoppable. Your **resilience** and **persistence** will be obvious to anyone who is lucky enough to cross your path. A story to illustrate this point:

I first met Kelly when I walked into her bread store about twenty years ago. Here was a tall, energetic young lady who was covered in flour, running around the store, making bread and stopping only occasionally to talk to an eager customer. She was proud of her bakery, a quaint new building she had built to resemble an old red barn. Her specialty was making the perfect loaf of bread, in many different types, with varying flavors . . . but with one main difference from what you'd typically find on a grocery store shelf. Her bread was pure. It was made as healthy as absolutely possible, using no artificial ingredients, colors, or chemicals. She sold it in small, not inexpensive loaves, and since it was preservative-free it had to be eaten within seven days. In short, her bread was amazing. And the customers came—in droves.

At the time I was writing this book, some twenty years later, I knew I wanted to tell Kelly's story. I sat down for an interview, expecting to hear some sophisticated tale of a woman who chased per passion for making the perfect bread. What I got was an entirely different story. While both of these versions would have ended the same way, it was the path of **persistence** that I had not expected when we first met. As a young girl of twelve, she was a somewhat wild child. She says she had the perfect mother, yet felt disconnected from her world. . . . Her father being an out-of-town oil worker, she had the freedom to do what she wanted, maybe even too much freedom, and she took good advantage of that. As with most teenagers, there were some rebellious times, some underage drinking, and just generally letting herself go a bit. As college approached, her father insisted she try to get a scholarship, which she did earn, but her partying got in the way of her studies, and she remembers feeling she was just going to college to make her father happy. But one thought remained constant in her mind. She wanted to make a good life for herself, her sisters, and her family. These thoughts **persisted**, more and more as time went on.

With school not taking her anywhere specific or satisfying, she bounced around, finding waitressing jobs to help with the bills. At age twenty-one, she married, and soon gave birth to twins. Visions of success, her own success, stayed in the front of her mind, however. She told me that at the time, she considered those visions her love language, that they were how she wanted her world (and those around her) to be. She would soon discover that her new husband was an alcoholic, and they divorced a few years later. Kelly returned to waitressing to help pay the bills and raise her children. She tells me that after a few years, she was promoted to bartender, in recognition of the friendly and kind service, and with it came a chance to spend more time with the regulars who came in often and stayed around late, sitting at the bar and pondering their lives.

A half-dozen years went by for her in that establishment. Customers would come and go, and things would change . . . all except those feelings she just couldn't seem to shake.

She told me that she remembered one gentleman, an older man who had a few successful businesses. He shared with her that what he really wanted to do was to open a bread store, something he had been thinking about and working on for some time. After months of discussion, he opened that bakery, with Kelly as the bread salesperson behind the counter. After some success, he offered her her own small retail store to manage, giving her incentives based on how much bread she could sell. She spent the next two years selling bread out of that store, making money, and seeing her life, the good life she had envisioned so many years earlier, begin to show itself. Empowered by the ability to control her own income, she went to any length to gain new customers. She remembers going to local tennis courts, golf courses, any public event she could find, handing out free samples of their now very popular bread.

Her **persistence** would be rewarded, as the owner was nearing retirement, recognized Kelly's potential, and gave her the opportunity to open her own store. Soon she was baking bread for herself, experimenting with different recipes, always tweaking the ingredients. And she persisted. She now had two growing boys to feed, and failure was not an option. No worries on that score. Business boomed, to the point that her small store just couldn't keep up. Offices, hospitals, and local businesses ordered her bread regularly, and she was selling it as fast as she could make it. To keep up with demand, she needed to expand, and quickly. She needed an investment, and so, in her usual **persistent** way, she approached a local bank to ask for a loan.

Now, anyone who knows anything about banking knows one thing. They have the money, and they don't part with it easily, especially to start-up companies. However, this is a lesson in persistence, after all. And so this is what Kelly did next. She laughs as she talks about the day she walked into that bank to ask for a loan to expand her business. She remembers the look on the faces of the bankers (all in suits) as she entered the local branch that early afternoon in her sweatpants, hair twisted up in a rubber band on top of her head, nothing in her hands, and covered head to toe in flour from that early morning's bake. She was promptly asked to show her business plan. "Where are your flow charts, revenue predictions, expense forecasts, and profit margins?" the banker asked her. "I have none of that stuff," she admitted sheepishly.

Not to be deterred, she did show them she had the one thing that no business can do without—demand. She explained that she had landed several large accounts, including firms like Chrysler and The Honey Baked Ham Company, each of which were ordering hundreds of loaves every week! All in, she was currently baking thousands of loaves to keep up with demand. She wasn't leaving, she persisted, and she walked out of that bank, loan approval in hand . . . no charts, no forecasts, no colorful graphs.

Today, she enjoys her new bakery, Country Grains, still pumping out trucks full of bread daily, while keeping the authenticity of a small-town general store. I still go there to this day to see Kelly, wish her well, and buy one of her amazing deli sandwiches. You'll soon learn that there are two kinds of people in this world—the doers and the dreamers. The only difference is the idea that drives them, and the attributes that follow that drive.

THE SOMEDAYERS AND THE TODAYERS CLUBS

When it comes to success and achievement, I have come to believe that people generally belong to one of two "clubs," or groups. I only caution you to be careful here because I have personally hung out at both of these clubs in my lifetime and I can tell you they are very different when it comes to achieving what you want to accomplish.

The names of these two clubs are the *Somedayers Club* and the *Todayers Club*. While the names may suggest the obvious, it is important to understand the subtle differences between the members of each club and how you and your goals can benefit from keeping them apart. Remember also that you have a choice as to which club you join.

THE SOMEDAYERS CLUB

The Somedayers Club has lots of members, but this club can never be full enough. The parking lot is packed with cars—man, it seems like the happenin' place—yet somehow, there's always room for more. Busloads of potential members arrive every day to join. The reason for such a large membership is that it's so darn welcoming and easy to get into. *Everyone is accepted! No background checks! There's no minimum payment or sacrifice!* Most join not even realizing that there's another club in town; they've heard only of this club because it's all they've ever known. Its location is so easy to find—there are no red lights, detours, or obstacles of any kind. The atmosphere inside the Somedayers Club is great. It seems so warm and safe—familiar. You'll soon discover many of the members' parents belong there too, as well as their parents' parents and even their cousins, friends, and classmates. The place is filled with people they know who are just like them! As they mingle about, they realize how well-intentioned everyone is. In fact, they see them standing around and hear them saying things like:

- *Someday I am going to start my own business.*
- *Oh yeah? Someday I'm going to start my own nonprofit!*
- *Sure, that's great and all, but someday I am going to take my family on a cruise around the world!*
- *Someday I'm going to build myself a dream home.*
- *Let's have lunch someday.*

- *Someday I'm gonna take that yoga class.*
- *Someday I'll open a 401(k).*

You can always tell which members have belonged to the Somedayers Club since a very young age. Whenever someone asked them what they wanted to be, what they wanted to do, or where they wanted to go when they grew up, they answered: "Someday, I'm going to be . . ." In fact, they practiced saying that so much, they just kept at it. And that's all it took; with just that line alone, they gained lifelong membership into the Somedayers Club. Sure, members are positive, fun folks with lots of good stories to share. And no doubt, anyone who arrives is immediately welcomed with enthusiasm and open arms. (FYI: While they'd love to be able to process your application immediately, they're likely to wait for optimal conditions, as they figure that most Somedayers are accustomed to "making do for the time being." In fact, that's the Somedayers Club's official motto: "Make do for now; I'm sure someday we'll get to it!")

Thinking about joining? Think again. Be careful, because once you're in, you're a lifetime member. As most members will attest, once you're there, it is very hard to leave. The reason is simple: everyone intends to leave "someday," but someday never comes. And members hate to see other members go. You'll come to learn that Somedayers will be willing to spend a lot of time and energy trying to convince you never to leave their team. They often have innumerable excuses why their friends shouldn't leave the Somedayers Club:

- *Do you know how much houses these days cost?*
- *What's the point in saving? I wanna have fun today, and who knows what tomorrow holds.*

- *Why start your own company? All those headaches? Stay where you are. It's safe!*
- *You'll have plenty of time to do it someday—when you have more money.*

Seriously, I've actually heard these arguments from plenty of well-intentioned folks—over and over, I might add. And every time I do, I want to jump out the window. I mean, I will never get that forty-five minutes of my life back—listening to people talk themselves out of their own future and success.

Here's the point: not only does this club cater to members who do nothing but dream about *living versus actually living*, they also have many members who don't want you to leave and join the other club. The pooh-poohing of your ideas is a way to keep you in, to hold you back. You might feel them hanging on to your shirt as you try to exit. "Don't go, we NEED you here with us!" they plead.

Most of us are not aware that we are living and working in places surrounded by Somedayers. We've all become so accustomed to hearing the word *someday* (even using the word ourselves) that we've become immune to it. And here's what happens to Somedayers. When they retire or at the end of their life, they are recognized with a special award, kind of like a Lifetime *Un*-Achievement Award. This award is *exclusively* for Regrets-Only Members. You've met members in your own circle, I'm sure, and you've heard their familiar words:

- *I should have left that dead-end job years ago.*
- *I should have started my own business.*
- *I could have done that if I'd tried, but I'll never know now.*
- *I should have taken that vacation.*

- *I should have paid more attention to my kids.*
- *I should have exercised more.*

Believe me, as a guy who's on the other side—the early years of hard work and perseverance have paid off, and I'm looking forward to a lot of fun and peaceful years ahead of me. Simply stated: there is no putting off your life. *Someday* comes and smacks you in the ass pretty fast. Your kids grow up and move out before you can blink. The thing you thought would take forever to achieve is just a distant memory. Life goes by fast. Don't let *someday* become *never*. Don't end up with the coveted Lifetime Un-Achievement Award, surrounded by people who wish they'd have done things differently. You deserve better than that. The world deserves better than that. I want to throw a better option your way. It's a club that requires you to act quickly and waste no time, and it's one you can join—today.

THE TODAYERS CLUB

One of the first things you'll notice about the Todayers Club is the parking lot. It has plenty of cars, but you quickly realize not nearly as many as in the Somedayers lot. Why? It's simple: it doesn't have as many members. What's important is the quality of its membership, not the quantity. And when you think of who you decide to surround yourselves with, your goal should be to have as many supportive and motivational people as possible. Take this seriously. Maybe it's true that you cannot choose your family, but let's be wise about who we choose to share our life goals with. It is critical that you connect with those who will be there for you while you walk your life path. These are the people who will put a hand on your shoulder to steady you when necessary.

Superficially, this club might not look all that different from the Somedayers Club. You'll see lots of small groups of people having conversations with one another. Everything seems in order. Folks are generally happy and enthusiastic. But the energy is different, and you can feel it. Smiles abound and heads are held high. You just sense that this is a place you'd rather belong to. And your tour now begins.

You start to meet members and talk with them, but somehow the discussions you hear are quite different at this club. You sense a palpable absence of commiseration. Quite the opposite, actually. Their word choices are not the same. The answers to the questions being posed among them are positive and result-driven. The answer to "Let's have lunch sometime" is met by "I have my calendar open on my phone—how's next Tuesday?" and then, "Great, let's try that new sushi place, I'll see you there!" You're not hearing anyone discuss the *possibility* of opening a 401(k). No, instead you hear two people reviewing their growing investment portfolios with each other, excited about their future earnings. No one is thinking about *maybe* taking a yoga class *someday*. Nope, quite the contrary. The talk you hear is how great they are feeling after their first ten sessions, and as you listen further, they invite friends to meet them at class on Saturday morning.

These are folks who created a vision and a plan for their work life. Maybe it was to learn a trade or a skill that was in high demand. Maybe they had a plan to gain great experience with their skill and eventually open their own business. You'll probably hear about how that business expanded from a couple employees to a hundred or more, because they believed in an idea, took a calculated risk, and followed a specific plan. Certainly you'll hear about how they give back to their communities, based on their individual success, in the spirit of *to whom much is given, much is expected*. Finally, what you don't hear is a bunch of *hope talk* regarding the eventual purchase of a home or truck or vacation. The conversation is refreshingly different, in that one member proudly tells another he has hired a real estate agent to begin the search—down payment and bank pre-approval letter in hand.

You notice something else. This is a club full of doers. You put out a goal to this crowd, and they help you figure out how you can accomplish it, plain and simple. Your life ideas, no matter how lofty, aren't shot down just so the shooters can feel better about their ineffective selves. This is a place that doesn't need an overabundance of members. The Todayers would love to have you, but if you don't join them then, unlike the Somedayers, they simply hope the best for you in whatever you decide.

I think the greatest part about being a member here is that the others have good memories. They will hold you accountable to meet your goals. They will ask for updates to confirm you're steady on your path. They will check on you along the way. They will be there with you, and when you finish, they will be proud of your accomplishments, no matter how large or small. Finally, they will share in your pursuit of comfort, peace, and freedom.

1. Take a moment and think about the two clubs as they relate to your own life and those around you. What club have you been hanging out in? What club do you identify most with? How about your friends and family?

Can you place them in one club or the other? I'll leave space below so that you can actually write the answer here.

2. Name one thing you've said you'll do someday. What small step can you take to make that someday—today?

3. Name one thing you've said you'd do that you've already accomplished. How did that make you feel? Did you have any support? Did anyone help you achieve your goal?

4. Identify at least three people who you think will help you accomplish whatever goals you set out for yourself.

In the previous pages of this book, you took some time to really picture and visualize the life you wanted for yourself. I asked you to see it clearly in your mind. Take a moment right now to again bring to mind the image of the life you see yourself living. *It's pretty sweet, right?* Maybe you even discussed it a bit over at the Somedayers Club with some of your friends: "I've always dreamed that *someday . . .*" Well, *my goal* in this chapter has been to help you make that someday dream into a reality once and for all. The entire purpose of this book is to help you walk down a path that will take you there. It won't come all at once. At first, you'll achieve small wins, then you'll be able to achieve two or three at a time, and before you know it, you'll be achieving bigger and bigger wins. I hope you enjoy your membership in the Todayers Club! You will become a goal-crushing machine.

10

REMEMBERING WHAT IS IMPORTANT— GIVE, GET, AND GIVE AGAIN

I am going to propose something radical in this final chapter, so it may take you some time to digest. You may even doubt the wisdom of it, because for your entire life, your circle of influence has told you something very different. This is one of those times where you just have to trust the messenger as well as the message, mostly because the masses will try to convince you that what I am about to tell you goes against popularly held beliefs, and therefore simply can't be true. I am going to ask you to remember what is important in life, even if you have to think outside the box to understand what I'm saying. So here goes: don't define your life by your career or how you spend your working days. I repeat: *Do not define your life's happiness by what you do for a living.* Instead, I'd like you to define your life by *what you do WITH what you do for a living.* Let that sink in for a minute. This is important to remember as you start down the path toward a life of comfort, peace, and freedom.

Let's focus on this option for you when it comes to defining your life and all it can encompass. This option is representative of what I consider to be truly important in life. I'm talking about your gifts, and the fact that they should be discovered, nurtured, developed, and honed sharp . . . and then shared with the rest of the world.

Wait a minute, you're probably thinking, *I bought this book because it's about choosing a career I love, and now you're telling me my career is secondary to my happiness?*

Exactly right, and kudos to you for pointing that out, but please just bear with me while I explain. You see, being successful, providing for your family, and building a great life are all within reach. And all of this is even more within your grasp, if you keep perspective on what is most important—pride from a job well done, involvement in your community, and giving back of your time, your money, and your internal gifts. You don't have to be a corporate titan, a pop star, or a professional athlete.

Let me guess. You've probably heard these bromides from your friends, your family, and maybe even the inspirational posts sent to you on social media:

- *Climb that corporate ladder.*
- *Do what you love and the money will follow.*
- *You are what you do.*
- *Never stop chasing your dreams.*

You've heard these pithy little sayings before, right? Here's the bone I have to pick with them. They're great in theory, but in reality, they're not always the best advice.

Let's look at one area where this kind of advice is terrible. Did you ever notice how many parents think their child is going to be the next star professional athlete? Camps, schools, and sidelines are filled with parents and coaches telling kids: *Follow your dream! You want to be an NFL player—just don't give up! You can do it.* You never hear anyone lean in to the coach of a small-town high school football team and whisper, "Maybe your interest in football should be to just follow your favorite team from your couch on Sunday and then get up on Monday and go to work for your dad in that mechanic shop of his. You'll have a great life." We don't remind kids that an extremely (and I mean, extremely!) small percentage of athletes, just nine of every ten thousand kids, will turn professional, nor do we tell them about the reality for those who do. Guess what? According to the NFL Players Association, the average NFL career is just 3.3 years! That begs the question . . . then what, retire rich? Nope. The reality there is that all the big money comes after year five in the NFL, if you make it that long. The very next reality is that of having to get a job that satisfies you in every way possible. To prove this point even further, let's not forget the research I previously cited about most college grads: upward of 43 percent don't end up working in the field they went to college to study.

I know a lot of people who went to school with a very fixed mind-set about what they wanted to do in life and what they wanted to achieve, and were sorely disappointed when life didn't turn out exactly as they had planned when they were a mere eighteen years old. I've met plenty of negative, bitter, and resentful people who in their fifties and sixties are still complaining about their lost dreams, lack of money, or dissatisfaction with their career. In my mind, this is usually the result of the practice of waiting for life to happen to them, instead of clearly planning for the life they desired. Remember the study I cited earlier that showed that 80 percent of us admit to not having any real-life goals. That's a lot of people just floating through this world with no real direction.

The feeling that something better or more amazing was available to us in the past if only we had succeeded at a singular career moment is a common predicament. On the other side of the coin, however, the happiest and most fulfilled people I know have fallen in love with the work at hand *by doing* the work at hand as a means to a positive end. They stayed focused on the job in front of them, but did so as a way of getting their envisioned life going, not the other way around. They became experts at the process through a lot of hard work, and they ultimately succeeded. They shared their individual gifts with the world.

Too often, people blur the idea of their purpose in life with their careers or how they earn their money. It's come to the point that there are a lot of people walking around this planet thinking that how much money they have in the bank is a direct correlation to how much they're worth as a human being. And they think this regardless of how they actually feel while out in the world or what their level of comfort, peace, and freedom might be. This seems to be okay if your wallet is constantly flush, but what happens when things aren't going so great and you've come upon some tough times? Or what if you were born with nothing? Does that mean you're worthless as a human being?

Nope, sorry, I don't buy it. But chances are, *you* might—at least on a subconscious level. I think I've made it clear that I am not a doctor. Nor did I spend years in college poring over longitudinal studies of human behavior. But you don't have to be a Nobel Prize winner in science to point out the obvious: lots of humans are running around and around in the rat race because they think that what they do or how much they earn determines their worth. Humans can be slaves to the dollar. It's become a calling card of sorts: *I have money, therefore I am.*

Right now, so many young people are going through the motions by falling into debt to afford a fancy pedigree school, then showing up at jobs they dislike. For this very reason, they think that where they went to school, their corporate title, or the magnitude of their bank statement determines their humanity, regardless of how happy (or unhappy) they actually feel. But don't lose heart. You're not going to be one of these people. You know better now, as Oprah says, so you're going to do better. You've become aware of this human tic, and so now you're less likely to mindlessly follow the pack of lemmings running straight off the cliff.

Let's be honest. You can be the richest guy on the planet, but if your riches are born of greed and deceit, then who really cares? I know a lot of rich people, and some of them are miserable, believe me. No one is better than anyone else. Whether you're digging for barrels of oil or septic tanks, it doesn't make a bit of difference. Who you truly are is not measured by how much you earn, but rather who you are at the core and how able you are to give the best parts of you away to others. And I'll say it again: it doesn't matter what your last name is or where you're from or what type of upbringing or limitations you began with, you can always give something to this world and the people in it. Each of us possesses a **gift** that the rest of us can't wait to see.

MY SUPERPOWER, MY GIFT

I believe our purpose in life—yours, mine, everyone's—is to discover our true **gifts** and then find a way to use them to help others and make the world a better place. That's it. That's what we're here to do: *Figure out what we have, then give away that unique **gift** to others.*

My job is president of Rusk Industries Inc. It's a dirty business with jackhammers and concrete, buckets of tar, and tons of gravel. But I love my job, love the people I work with, and love having a business I can call my own. Yet with all its challenges, the most satisfying part of my job is helping others find and complete their goals, start walking that path and see it through to its completion, all the while enjoying the ride. I guess you could say that through all the dust and construction, I discovered my true **gift**. In my case, it was the ability to help people see their future and guide them along the way. It was a "job" that I relished completely.

A few years ago, during our company's weekly goals meeting, a woman in our office admitted that she wanted to focus on the goals she had envisioned in her head, but felt stuck behind a pile of bills. Turns out several thousand dollars were being taken from her wages for an old apartment lease (with an old boyfriend) that had come back to haunt her. She then revealed to me that for the past two winters she had been driving to and from work with a broken heater. Her dream, she told me, was to be free from the heavy burden of debt. She also hoped one day to take a vacation with her kids to Florida to see her aging mother.

I told her she needed to build a plan that would make absolutely certain she would arrive at that dream. And so we did. We created a savings plan that would eliminate her debts over a ten-month period. Once that was no longer an issue, she was able to put the same money toward a new car heater. Once the heater was repaired and paid for, she immediately began saving for a trip to Florida to see her mother. That goal took a little longer to achieve, but once the path was set, she stuck it out. Ultimately, she achieved all three goals within sixteen months! And the best part? She now visits her mother every year, has built up her savings, *and* has shed the stress, fear, and anxiety of all that debt. She replaced it with—you guessed it—comfort, peace, and freedom.

I have helped many people who are creating amazing lives for themselves and their families without going into burdensome debt, and most important, without dreading their daily grind. It's a lot easier to love what you do and enjoy doing it, no matter what it is, when it allows you to achieve the things that matter to you most. And as I have said many times—anyone can do it!

Have you ever caught yourself saying this?

- *But I don't make enough money.*
- *I can barely survive on what I earn now.*
- *I already have so much debt and work so hard.*
- *I just can't get ahead in this economy.*
- *Easy for you to say; you're the boss of your own business.*
- *I only make $12 an hour.*
- *I can't afford my rent, have two kids in day care, don't receive child support, and have to care for my aging parents.*

Man, I hear you. Life is hard, and there is no shortage of curveballs. I get it. I seriously do. But I'm here to give you hope that you can turn it around. You heard me right: no matter what your situation, you can turn it all around.

This is going to sound harsh, but I think it's necessary. Only *you* are responsible for your life and your outcomes. I truly believe that with the right mind-set, you can and will achieve anything you put your mind to. If you no longer want to make $12 an hour, then don't. I assure you there is a job out there that pays more. Go find it. Figure out what you need to do to be prepared. Be willing to step outside your comfort zone and pursue another kind of work. Then stay the course and improve your skills every day on the job. Most important, stay positive and open to the opportunities that come your way. The only way you can do that is by staying on the path. One that only YOU can set for yourself.

I've seen seemingly impossible and hopeless cases in my day. I've seen people who were down and out and had no hope left in them and who still managed to turn their lives around. I think of my buddies Mark, Jim, and Tim. I've seen many others like them, but I shared their stories because I can't think of more resilient, positive, and vision-oriented people. Mark Martin, if you'll remember, was on his own at eighteen years old, having to care and provide for his brothers. He had lost everything—most important, his beloved mother. But did that stop him? Hell, no. Remember Jim Moline? He was a hopeless, self-destructive addict. He was broke and had nothing. But that's just where he *started*. Look where he is *today*: owner of a successful construction company. And what about Natalia. Her path was set, but it wasn't the path she wanted for herself, so she left medical school and followed her passion. And then there's Tim Despoth, who didn't think he would ever be able to dig himself out of his enormous debt, but he did. And you can too. These people, and millions more, found their **gifts**, developed them, perfected them, and then shared them with the world.

When I first started to counsel employees who came to me with serious financial or other issues, I never really gave much thought to the advice I was giving them. I was just handing out bits of wisdom and tried-and-true methods that had worked for me—like setting goal paths and imagining with clarity the life I desired. But soon, without my even realizing it, ten people turned to twenty, and twenty turned to a hundred. One after another, they asked me to help them:

- *I need to pay off this horrible bill. I don't want to wait tables forever.*
- *I'm sick of fixing this old car.*
- *I've always dreamed of visiting my family in Europe.*
- *I'm tired of renting; I really want to own my own home.*
- *I think I need to get my scoliosis looked at.*
- *I have talents and passions that I think I'm ignoring.*

Every person who came to me knew the path they wanted to take. They had a good idea of what they wanted out of life; they just needed someone to guide them and help them get there. In the process, they had other realizations—that they were actually good at something. And then that something turned into another something, and another. Soon they were finding **gifts** they didn't know they had.

I realized then and there that *my* **gift** was helping others locate theirs. It was about helping others find their true life's path. I had been given so much, and now I could give back. *More aptly, I was free to give back.* Nothing was keeping me from sharing my **gifts**. I had attained comfort, peace, and freedom, and I wanted to pay it forward to everyone I met. I wanted them to feel what I feel every day, all day. And the funny thing was, the more comfort, peace, and freedom I seemed to share and give away, the more of it I received in return. It's never-ending. My world had never been this clear. I had discovered what it meant to be truly free; in fact, I had learned what it meant to be comfortable, peaceful, and free.

FINDING YOUR SUPERPOWER

So here's the big question: What do *you* have to give? Finding your **gift** is easier said than done. There is a lot at play when we start down the path toward finding our true talents. Some of us are raised in encouraging environments. Perhaps you're one of the lucky ones whose parents saw something amazing in you right away and decided then and there they would do anything in their power to help you succeed. Or perhaps you are an incredible athlete, artist, musician, or baker. Good for you! That's awesome. Chances are you're still enjoying these **gifts** that your parents encouraged to grow within you. We're the only ones who can limit who we become and what we do.

If you're like most of us, however, then knowing what your gifts really are can be a bit of a struggle. In some ways, we've been programmed to wonder if we're good at *anything*, thanks to this thing called *comparison*. Yes, we are always measuring ourselves against someone or something, in which case you're always asking yourself questions like, *Is someone a better athlete? A better problem solver? A better musician?*

Yes, someone is always better. Someone is always more educated, a better thinker, a faster worker, better at financial matters. Comparisons are truly, as they say, the thief of joy. We fill our bucket heads with this nonsense. We see someone excel at something we once thought we were pretty good at and we think, *Ah man, that could never be me.* So we stop. We say, "Why bother?" But you might want to rethink that.

- *Do you think we'd have a Tiger Woods if he saw Jack Nicklaus and he was like, "I could never be that good, so why even try?"*
- *Would there be a Tesla if Elon Musk said, "Cars? Yeah, can't compete with that"?*
- *Would there be an Apple computer if Steve Jobs saw an IBM machine and said, "Well, that's already been done!"*
- *What if Steven Spielberg said to himself at an early age, "Make movies? Nah, Francis Ford Coppola nailed that already."*

The truth is that everyone has their own talents, and yes, some of us share the same ones. But there is room for everyone to use their own. And use them we must. Why? Because the world needs us. You have amazing talents and skills that I don't, while at the same time I can offer things that you cannot. Together, we can do a lot. We can make the world better, both our own and everyone else's. It's that simple. My thinking has always been that giving of our true selves, giving of our unique **gifts**, is real freedom. And by the way, it feels fantastic.

FINDING SOMEONE WHO CAN HELP

Not long ago I signed up for an adventure at the New River Gorge national park. For those who have never been to or heard of the New River Gorge, it's a spectacular area of the country where one of the oldest rivers in North America rips and roars through lush West Virginia mountains. All along the river are abandoned mines, where at one time great American laborers toiled to keep the coal fires burning. It's a veritable wonderland for families and thrill seekers alike. You can do anything there—camp, hike, fish, hunt, climb on a high-ropes course or rocks, zip-line, and yes, of course, even go white-water rafting. In fact, it's world renowned for its "colossal rapids," which range in difficulty from class I to class IV, meaning from a calm water-park float to a truly terrifying down-river adventure. Owners of white-water rafting companies are pretty clear on their websites (as are the many waivers you sign declaring that you will not hold the company responsible for death or injury) that these rapids are not a Disney water ride. You can be sliced open by jutting rocks, be slammed into large boulders, fall out of the raft and be sucked under the powerful currents, cross-currents, or something they call "hydraulics," not to mention be frightened out of your mind.

Sounds like a good time.

So, of course, I paid my fees, signed my life away, got my paddle (who wants to be stuck up a river without a paddle?), life jacket, and helmet, and headed down the mountain in a school bus with a bunch of other intrepid spirits. On the bus, we listened as our river guide warned us of all the perils and dangers that lay ahead. He also let us know there was no shame whatsoever if any of us decided to stay on the bus and ride it back up the mountain without ever getting in the raft. Usually, one or two people on every bus bail, our guide reported.

Better to bail than to be impaled.

Getting on a raft and heading down a river with so many unknowns is not for the faint of heart. Those of us who decided to stay received a few quick instructions before being launched into the relatively tame part of the river—the calm before the storm, so to speak.

The river guide did not come to play. He was all business. He had his game face on. "One wrong move and you're dead," he was basically telling us. *Okay, then.*

While still in the calm waters, our guide taught us how to brace our feet and wedge them in where the side of the raft meets the bottom. *Uh, wait, there are no straps holding us onto this thing?* He taught us how to paddle and how necessary it was to work together. All we had to do was follow his lead. He would shout out what to do, and we would do it. He taught us the best way to hold the paddle, and then he said something fascinating: "Let the river do the work. It's just going one way." The river was going one way. We weren't going to be paddling against it. We just had to get down the river—from the drop-off location to the pickup location—without getting killed.

So if we were just going to let the river take us, what the hell did we need a river guide for?

Well, within about five minutes the answer to that became very clear. The river guide told us where to direct our paddles. We followed his instructions, and sure enough, we didn't crash into that giant boulder the river was directing us toward. Our guide had been negotiating this river for more than twenty years. He knew the location of every large rock, and where the currents would pull or push us. He knew when we were going to drop, and how the boat would react when it did. He'd been there before. Many times. And he could see what lay ahead before any of us novices.

The guide took us on an exhilarating ride and showed us that we were capable of doing things we never thought possible. He pointed out special skills that each of us had and worked with us so that the team on the raft operated with maximum efficiency. He also told the occasional joke and made sure we enjoyed the journey.

In the end, we arrived at our destination. We all felt so proud of what we had been able to do individually and what we had accomplished working together. Sure, the river took us where it wanted us to go, but we each did our part to steer the raft without disaster to its ultimate destination.

You may be thinking, *Where is he going with all this?* Guess what? You're on a river ride right now. It's the ride of your life. It's game on. And it's only traveling in one direction. The second you were born, you were moving toward your ultimate destination. The thing is, there are a lot of boulders, harsh currents, and jutting rocks that can wound us pretty badly if we're not careful. Some of us are so scared, we never even get on the stinkin' boat. We'd rather bail than fail. We watch from the sidelines. We let others take the licks for us. The rest of us are just floating along and need some direction. Sometimes we need a course correction and sometimes we need a river guide, someone who knows what's up ahead because he's been there before and can teach us what we don't know. We need someone who's going to push us to our maximum capacity of human potential. And maybe we need someone who cares enough about us to avoid having us end up impaled on a rock.

If you're stuck, if you feel like you're spinning in an endless eddy going nowhere fast, you need to call on a guide, someone who knows something about you, about your dreams, where you're headed, and what you want out of life. Those guides are going to see things in you that you can't see for yourself. They know your strengths; they know the potential that exists inside you, and they want to see you succeed. Remember the goal.

You are looking for the freedom of being fully aware of and actively giving of your true gifts.

Sure, many of you may be thinking: *I don't need anyone! I am good! I can rely on my many positive character traits and the open mind-set that I've just accepted!* Well, good for you. I like that kind of confidence, but in reality, no one achieves success on their own. Besides being a motivated, hardworking, and ethical individual who possesses a positive, can-do attitude, you're also going to need some friends, mentors, and supporters to walk that path with you. Your success will count on it, so please pick your *path partners* with that thought in mind.

So here's my advice: Find someone who can help you, then find someone you can help in the same way. And don't let that cycle end. There is so much power in giving, more than you will ever know.

GENEROSITY—TO WHOM MUCH IS GIVEN, MUCH IS EXPECTED

By now I think you understand that one of the driving forces behind the profiles of unconventional heroes included in this book is not just their career paths, but also their character traits, regardless of their particular career. The nature of their character has been a driving force in their lives and the reason they were able to push forward in pursuit of who they ultimately wanted to become. I shared these character traits (and the people I know in my life who personally exhibited them) not only to inspire you to discover your own special qualities but also to show you that no matter where you start out in life, you can achieve amazing things if you access the resilience, simplicity, persistence, faith, initiative, vision, courage, and **generosity** that we *all* have the possibility to possess.

We've already discussed, in no particular order of relevance or importance, the basic character traits I believe empower individuals to ultimately achieve anything in life, no matter where they get their start. But I have one more attribute to tell you about—the single character trait I believe makes all others possible. It's *generosity*.

Like always, let's start with the dictionary definition of *generosity*—"The quality of being kind and generous." And *generous*? It's defined simply as a person "showing a readiness to give more of something, as money or time, than is strictly necessary or expected." There's more to this, however—much more. It may seem like a paradox, but I can attest that the more you give, the more you receive. I am not just talking about money; I am talking about everything, and I mean *giving* everything of yourself. I don't think people fully understand or realize the power that comes from giving. The more you give—of your time, your service, your skills, your talents, your trust, your goodness, your courage, your vision, your persistence, your faith—the more you will receive those things in return, and then some. Your good works, deeds, and donations will pay dividends. True **generosity** begins in the heart, and shows itself without expectation of a return. Please remember that as we go forward.

And here's the thing: You don't have to be a well-to-do person to be a caring, giving one. You just have to be willing to give of yourself, of your time, or even a little bit of each to realize the power of **generosity**.

The person who taught me the most, and at the earliest age, about this power is my mother, Ginger. Before my dad made it "big," he was an entry-level grocer trying to raise five boys on a small salary. Needless to say, Mom didn't have a lot to work with to try to feed our family, let alone shop for herself or splurge on anything fancy. I recall one store we used to shop at regularly was called Goodwill. My brothers and I didn't know the difference between Goodwill and the local department store.

Though my mother didn't have a lot of money to give away, she showed us in many other ways what it means to be **generous**. She showed me that no matter how little you have in life, you always have enough to share. I clearly remember her offering bologna sandwiches to my neighborhood friends and never letting anyone leave hungry. I remember her making us homemade pizzas because we couldn't afford to order them, even from a fast-food pizza chain. Thanks to Mom's kindness and ingenuity, we boys never knew that Dad was struggling to make ends meet. She never let on that we were what other people might call "poor"—living on a grocer's $14,000 annual salary. We had what we thought was a pretty normal childhood. My mom was an amazing homemaker. She created a happy, safe, and wonderful place for my brothers and me to grow up. She supported my father's goals and career, and did everything possible to keep the home fires burning while he was off working seventy hours a week to move his way up in the world. She never complained. She was **generous** in deed and spirit.

Most important for me personally, during all my facial surgeries and dental visits and the many painful recovery days that came with them, my mother was my rock. She stood by me, took care of me, supported me, and kept reminding me that though I didn't look exactly like the other kids, I was no less special, no less worthy, no less capable of accomplishing anything I put my heart and mind to. Mom didn't need a college degree to be a kind and decent person, a good and **generous** human being. She just *was* one. She taught me early and often that not everyone has equal advantages. She taught me compassion. She taught me perspective. She taught me to lead by example.

My mom married a tough-as-nails, booming, demanding, and charismatic marine. That might harden a lot of people, but not Mom. She was in so many ways the rose to his thorns. She taught me the softer side of achieving one's goals. She taught me how to pay attention to people's needs, to listen to *their* stories, *their* goals, *their* dreams. That was *her* superpower, and I wanted it to be mine. In many ways, I believe so many people come to me to share their visions and goals because I listen. My mother taught me how to do that. She always listened to me and to others. It takes a **generous** person to give your time to someone else and listen—just to be there for them. And my mother was always there for me, and for anyone who needed her.

I believe the foundation my mother gave me early on is what drives my desire to give back. Many years ago, when my daughter was suffering from her disease, a friend of a friend approached me with the offer of paying for all our transportation costs to and from the various hospitals we visited those first few weeks. He was a man I barely knew, yet he stepped up with what eventually cost him a lot of money. I remember asking him at the time why he would do something like that, something so **generous**, for someone he hardly knew. I'll never forget what he told me that terrible afternoon. He said, "To whom much is given, much is expected." That powerful statement has stuck with me, to be sure. And along with the lessons my mother taught me, his random act of kindness is what drives all the charitable things I do to this very day. My company and its employees give not only our funding, but our time, volunteering, supporting, and attending events at over twenty charities each year.

No matter where you are in life, no matter what your financial situation, you can give. If you can't give your money, then give your time. Lord knows we need all the help we can get out there. Even if you just take the time to listen. Your listening tools, your ears and what they can mean to others, are just as powerful as cash, if not more. I have had hundreds of sit-downs where all I did was listen and care. Those experiences are powerful, and the feeling you get from them is unmatched.

It's hard to drive this point all the way home because I don't think enough people realize just how much being generous can bring meaning to your life. **Generosity**, in my mind, is just another form of gratitude. It's the active form. It's not just saying, "I am grateful for this life and all that I have in it." It is *showing* the world how grateful you are. I truly believe if you want to achieve anything in life, you need to start from that place. By being grateful for every job, every moment, every advantage, or even every hardship and obstacle that teaches you something new, you'll be able to achieve anything you draw with your Crayola crayons. Most important, you'll be able to recognize comfort, peace, and freedom when you see it . . . and you'll be so grateful that you won't be able to contain yourself. You'll want to share it with others. You'll want to give of your gifts. . . . Giving—it does a body good.

IN SUMMARY

Okay, this is it. This is the last time I'll be speaking to you (apart from in your head, of course). So listen clearly now. Really focus!

Discover your gift to the world because your unique gift IS your river! There is a freedom in following that path. You don't have to think too much.

You get to wake up and know where you're headed and what you're doing. You get to use that amazing mind of yours. It has enormous power—it pushes you instead of you pushing it. It meanders through your life, carrying you on its way. And don't forget that heart of yours. Follow where your curiosities lead and where your talents and gifts take you. That's the only way you can share your gifts with others.

I also hope that by now you realize that the more you share, the more you'll receive in return. You don't have to donate a million bucks to *feel* like a million bucks. In fact, in order to *feel* like a million bucks, just give away a small piece of yourself. Share a talent or a skill. Help someone in need. Give a bit of your time for a cause that means a lot to you. Do something that will make a difference in someone else's life.

Whatever you do, don't stay on the bus. Jump into the boat you call life and keep paddling. You're going to get to your ultimate destination no matter what you do, but why not get there with friends you've helped along the way, with appreciation for the guides that helped you, and with the knowledge that you have permission to do anything you want in life?

So one last time, dig in:

- What are your special gifts and talents? How do you think you can use them to give back to others?

- What do you do that makes you feel most alive? Who can you share that enthusiasm with?
- Identify a "river guide" in your life. Who can you count on to give you advice that will point you in the right direction? Have you thanked this person lately?
- Have you ever helped someone or guided someone before? How did it make you feel?
- Identify someone in your life who you can help. What can you do to help them realize *their* special gifts and talents and get them to where they want to go?

Finally, I hope you can see that no matter where you are today, you have the qualities within you to accomplish whatever you desire. And if you don't know what it is that you want or can do, I hope this chapter, this book, has offered you some possibilities that were otherwise unknown or not revealed to you. I hope you can see that there is more to life than good grades or getting into college or making a lot of money. And I also hope you can see that you can make a decent living—and yes, even for some of you, a lot of money—without going to college. I did name this book *Blue-Collar Cash*, after all. Please understand that there is PLENTY of opportunity in this world to create a life of comfort, peace, and freedom without a college education. I hope you feel at ease enough now to move out of your comfort zone and start exploring all sorts of different, albeit unconventional, paths that await you. Remember, you possess the positive traits I've mentioned. Which ones do you feel are most dominant in you?

I'd like to thank you for spending some time with me on this first journey toward a better, more complete life, one filled with comfort, peace, and freedom. It has been my honor to have shared not only what I have learned over the past few decades, but to have shown you how you can harness this knowledge to create your own desired world. If I've been successful, you are now able to look at the world in a new and exciting way. You are armed with the tools to see your future, to document that vision, and to walk toward its successful conclusion. You can now see the potential in a life of passion, of new choices—choices that include the honor of working with your hands. And you can prosper in the blue-collar world because you've done this before in your mind, you've built your future with certainty, and you've shared your path with others who support you. And when and only when you have done that, you can then share your unique gifts with the world. I believe in you. . . . You got this!

ONE LAST STORY

On a final note: I recently learned an interesting fact about having pets. It has been discovered that having a pet can extend your life by a whopping 24 percent! That is amazing, to say the least. It can mean the difference between living until seventy instead of ninety or more. Wow. They say it has something to do with the easing of stress, and the activity surrounding the care and entertainment of a loving animal. Who knew? In the spirit of this new information, and being a dog and cat owner myself, I thought I would include a few thoughts on why having an animal can bring you loads of comfort, peace, and freedom. Read on and I hope you enjoy this final story.

Not long ago, Nancy, Nicole, and I lost our two golden retrievers, Max and his sister Sandy, within two months of each other. They had been our best friends and most loyal guardians for nearly fourteen years. Nicole looked upon them as her brother and sister, many times subjecting them to all different kinds of loving treatment, including costumes and even hair coloring. Needless to say, this was a tough loss for us all.

Sandy, one of the prettiest and most loving animals ever, was the first to pass away. We had arranged for her to have a minor procedure while we were out of town. Being an older dog, she took a turn for the worse. After we endured a painful long-distance phone call and an all-night drive back to the vet, the decision was made to euthanize her right away.

Max's passing was something altogether different. He was our rock. He seemed indestructible, even in old age. A huge dog with an imposing stare, he had dodged cancer, bad hips, and stomach issues, and had endured multiple surgeries after eating things he never should have. After Sandy's death, however, it was clear his ailing body could no longer support what his sharp mind wanted it to do. Though we heard nary a complaint, we could tell just by looking at him he was in pain, due in part to worsening arthritis and other ailments. We didn't want him to suffer any longer, so we made the difficult decision to let him go. Needless to say, it was one of the most uniquely powerful experiences of our lives, so intense, I think, because of the tsunami of emotions that bombarded us all at once. Unless you've gone through this experience yourself, it's truly difficult to aptly describe, but I'll give it my best shot.

Unlike with Sandy's demise, we were standing beside Max when he was put down. In fact, we were holding his ninety-three-pound body in our arms, while he slowly and peacefully drifted off to sleep, heading to his final resting place. And so there we were, holding our buddy, feeding him his treats, re-

membering our happy times with him, and giving him all the
love we possibly could. Thankfully, Max was no longer in pain.
He gave us one last look and a heavy sigh and then left to be
back with his sister.

All told, it took just fifteen minutes from the time the vet
administered the first calming shot to the moment of his peaceful passing. A blink. A dash. It seemed improbable and impossible. And yet it happened. Sandy was gone, and now Max. It felt
like every memory had been instantaneously erased, and yet at
the same time, had become crystal clear and fully in focus. In
fact, it seemed like only yesterday we had brought Max and his
sister home to meet their "sister," our daughter, Nicole, who
was just a little girl at the time.

These animals were calm, extremely curious, outwardly
kind, loving, playful yet disciplined, and just plain beautiful.
They became so entwined within our family that I could barely
conjure up a memory without them or Nicole. They were by
our sides wherever we went. They followed us from room to
room, sat by our feet while we watched television, or waited
quietly under the kitchen table while we ate dinner. At night,
they would follow Nicole upstairs, jumping into her bed for
the night, Sandy lying across the foot of the bed, Max sleeping up by Nicole, many times letting her use him as a pillow.
They were nearly human in their habits. Looking back on those
moments, it was clear they are some of the fondest memories
of our lives. And to think it almost didn't happen. We almost
didn't get these wonderful dogs.

When Nicole was four or five, Nancy and I decided she was
old enough to take on the responsibility of caring for a dog,
so we did some research in the hopes of finding just the right
breed for our family. I say WE researched the dogs, but the

process was spearheaded by Nicole, beginning with us purchasing a rather large dog book. Imagine a five-year-old girl carrying around a twenty-pound, full-color dog encyclopedia. It wasn't long before she could recite different breeds' sizes, body weights, exercise requirements, behavior patterns—you name it, she knew it. After several months of scientific-like research, four pads of Post-it notes, some advice from her aunt Cathy, and several debates, a decision was made. A golden retriever it would be.

In time, we would discover a reputable, multiple-generation breeder only thirty minutes from our home. I mentioned Nicole's aunt Cathy because she had some experience with the breed and was actually looking for a female herself. She asked us to keep an eye out for one to bring home for her. Now we were searching for two female dogs—one for us and one for Aunt Cathy. We made a few trips to look at the puppies, and by the time we made it back to pick up our two, the litter was down to three remaining puppies.

I picked up our two new ones, settled up with the breeder, and loaded our new kids into the truck. I was about to be on my way when I heard a small whimper behind me. I turned to look, only to discover the final member of the litter looking at me with a rather confused expression on his face. With those sad little eyes, he almost seemed to be saying, *What about me? You just gonna leave me here?* My mind began to race when I looked over to Nancy, who was starting to give me the very same look. Well, I suppose you can all guess what happened *next*.

I walked back to inspect this little fellow (mistake number one), a clumsy male with a small body but a big square head. I lifted him up in my arms (mistake number two) and held him while he licked my face. I looked at my wife again (mistake number three). I was done. "All right . . . put him in the truck," I moaned while I fished several hundred more dollars out of my pocket.

Looking back, I realize now what a fortunate and nearly accidental set of circumstances it was that brought Max into our lives. On the final day of his life, we thanked God for the time we'd had with both dogs. We thanked Max and Sandy for spending their lives with us. They had no doubt brought us a lifetime—fourteen years, in fact—of comfort, peace, and freedom.

So here's what I want you to take away from this story, and from this book. First, you will find that spending time in the company of an animal—whether going for a nice long walk down a wooden path in the park on a sunny Saturday morning or just catching a movie on the couch with your little best friend sleeping next to you—to be one of the most peaceful things you can ever do. But even more important than that, at the end of the day, what really matters in life has zero to do with where you went to school, what you do for a living, or how you "identify" yourself. It only matters that you love and were loved. That's it. That's what's going to give you the most peace, the most comfort, the most freedom. And you don't need a degree to figure that out, to do it, or to feel it. You don't need financial success either. You just have to love and be loved. You have to care for someone or something more than yourself—whether it's your wife, your husband, your child (or several children), a dog, a cat, a bird, a llama, a neighbor, a friend, an aunt or uncle, or your parents, doesn't matter a lick. *It only matters that you do it.* You have to keep it all in focus—why you're doing what you're doing. I realized this on a very deep level while holding Max in my arms and watching him drift from this life.

Here's the thing you already know, but probably really hasn't sunk in yet: *We only get one life here.* That's it. In a blink of an eye, it's over. We waste so much time and money worrying about so many things that in the end don't matter a bit. And most people I know who have taken the same path as I have express the very same feelings. Think about it. When you look back at all the times you spent interacting with loved ones— family, friends, even pets—you are looking at some of the most peaceful, happy moments you will ever have. (You can probably guess that since Max and Sandy passed, the Rusk family has made a home for two new arrivals—Bella and Blue, our golden retriever pups. Oh yes, and a cat too, who we rescued, named Mojo.)

I wrote this book for people who are intent on finding a clear path to their own version of comfort, peace, and freedom. I outlined all the ways you can create a life for yourself that you are fully in control of, one that will be free of stress and financially sound, and will allow you to walk your path to your dreams. I spelled out in some detail the character traits you'll require to get through this life, as well as the mind-set and attitude that you'll need. I walked you through the best ways to plan and work toward your goals and solve any problem that comes your way. And I advised you on the best ways to use your time and give back to others. I talked about keeping what is important in perspective—what really matters, namely the people (and animals) you love.

All of this is to say, if you truly want peace, if you want tranquility, if you want to think clearly and be healthy, achieve your dreams, and be absolutely and totally free, then *love someone or something.* But start with yourself. Tell yourself you matter. Tell yourself you deserve a good life, and your family and kids do too. God didn't give us this amazing planet and all the things in it—like happy, beautiful children, playful and loyal dogs, flowers, trees, and all Earth's natural wonders, not to mention endless paths to walk, and, yes, the ability to create golf courses—if He didn't want us to enjoy all of it. We are here to love and find joy. We are here to use our gifts and talents to help serve others. We all play a role, and we all matter. No job is too lowly to matter in the service of one another. We are here to find and then explore our own unique paths. We are here to dig deeper and find our own purpose. Ultimately, I believe we're here each to walk our own path, which leads us to more fully experience comfort, peace, and freedom.

Finally, I want you to hear this: you are in charge of and in control of the YOU that you want to be. I know you can do it. I have watched hundreds of people I've mentored and advised do it. If you're nervous, scared, or can't get out of your five-gallon-bucket head, then join me on a path already in progress. I promise to be a resource to help now and in the future. Follow my blog and website, reach out and let me know what your goals are—what path you're on to get you there. I'll be here cheering you on.

I hope you find success, happiness, and joy in all that you do. I wish you a life of comfort, peace, and freedom—the only life you are meant to live.

ACKNOWLEDGMENTS

First, let me speak to all of you who have come to this message. I am honored to share my thoughts and ideas with you, the blue-collar workers of our great America. I feel a special kinship with you for these specific reasons: I am you. I see you. I have been where you are. It is a privilege to walk among you, and I sincerely thank you for helping make our country great.

To Kevin, Mary, and Adam, and everyone at Kevin Anderson and Associates. Thank you for all your shepherding throughout this process. Your strategy and guidance to a first-time writer was no less than awesome.

To John Mass, Celeste Fine, Anna, and everyone at Park & Fine Literary and Media for taking a shot in the dark, and believing in my story and in me. You made this new experience so amazing. Huzzah!

To my editor, Carrie Thornton, and Peter Kispert, Ben Steinberg, Kendra Newton, Heidi Richter, Allison Hinchcliffe,

Ploy Siripant, Liate Stehlik, and all the folks at Dey Street and HarperCollins Publishers. I am both humbled and honored to be in your most capable hands. This book would be nowhere without you, and I am eternally grateful for your mentoring, your leadership, and your passion.

To Mark, Jim, Art, Rob, Natalia, Tim, Minnesota, Kelly, and Kierrah. Thank you for allowing me to tell your stories in the hope that they will inspire others. You are living examples of how to do it right.

To my amazing wife, Nancy. You don't know how many times I have overheard you telling the story of how this book came about and I can see in your face how proud you are. You have loved and supported me for over thirty years now and I am so thankful. You are truly the love of my life, now and forever.

To my amazing daughter, Nicole. Thank you for allowing me to share your incredible bravery with the world. Your story is the genesis of this, my first book. Mom and I are incredibly blessed to have you in our lives, and we couldn't love you more. And now that you are away at school, have no fear—I am not leaving the refrigerator door open for too long.

To my awesome parents. Dad, thanks for passing your pursuit of perfection on to me. Even if at times I didn't want to bleach the whitewall tires over and over and over again . . . I now know why you pushed us so hard. Mom, your kindness through both good and bad times could never be forgotten. With five boys under nine years of age, you wore many hats—ER nurse, psychologist, short-order cook, bus driver, and teacher . . . and you wore all of them so well.

Finally, I have to mention my four brothers: Mike, Jim,

Steve, and Joe. Growing up being in the middle of the pack taught me many things: UFC refereeing, in-home damage minimization, non-detectable food-stain removal, plausible deniability, and evidence disposal. One would be amazed at what can be learned from a good pizza roll fight.

APPENDIX 1

POSSIBLE PATHS THAT DON'T REQUIRE COLLEGE DEGREES

Following is a list of possible paths that don't require college degrees, along with their average yearly salaries. However, that is not to say that the following don't require certification, training, or some intensive learning program. There are so many jobs now that you can train for without ever having to step foot on a college campus, but you still have to do your homework! Also, please note, this is by no means a comprehensive list. And I believe that we don't yet know about many of the jobs that will be available in the next ten years. Times are changing and so are the needs of employers. Be open and ready and adaptable. Show up on time, do the work and studying that is required, put your ten thousand–plus hours in, and keep a positive attitude, and I am sure you'll be successful no matter what path you choose to ultimately dig into!

AIRLINE ATTENDANT: $52,000

AIR TRAFFIC CONTROLLER: $108,000

ACTOR: $50,000 to $15 million (if you're Jennifer Lawrence!)

ARCHITECTURAL DRAFTER: $56,000

ARTIST: Varies

AUTOMOBILE BODY REPAIRER: $54,660

BABYSITTERS/NANNY: $30,000 to 60,000

BAKER: $47,000 to $77,000

BARTENDER: $15,000 to $70,000 (regionally)

BOOKKEEPER: $54,040

BRAND AMBASSADOR: $60,000

BRICKMASON AND BLOCKMASON: $56,930

CATTLE RANCHER: $60,000

CHEF: $53,000

COMMERCIAL PILOT: $67,500

CONSTRUCTION AND BUILDING INSPECTOR: $52,360

CONSTRUCTION MACHINE OPERATOR: $70,000

CONSTRUCTION MANAGER: $95,956

COSMETOLOGIST: $55,000

COURT REPORTER: $48,000

CRIMINAL INVESTIGATOR AND SPECIAL AGENT: $53,990

DETECTIVE: $68,820

DENTAL HYGIENIST: $68,000

DIAGNOSTIC MEDICAL SONOGRAPHER: $64,380

DISPATCHER: $52,000

DRYWALL TAPER: $52,490

ELECTRICAL POWER LINE INSTALLER AND REPAIRER: $58,030

ELECTRICIAN APPRENTICE: $48,250

ELECTRONIC TECHNICIAN: $56,000

ELEVATOR INSTALLER AND REPAIRER: $65,893

EXECUTIVE ASSISTANT: $54,000

FARMER: $58,845

FASHION DESIGNER: $64,530

FIRE FIGHTING AND PREVENTION SUPERVISOR: $58,902

FOREMAN (MASON CREW): $50,000

FOREST FIRE FIGHTING AND PREVENTION SUPERVISOR: $58,920

FORKLIFT OPERATOR: $47,000

GAS PLANT OPERATOR: $57,200

GLAZIER: $66,640

GOLF CADDY: $52,000

HAIRSTYLIST: $40,000 to $80,000

HEATING AND REFRIGERATION MECHANIC: $43,000

ILLUSTRATOR: $60,000

IMMIGRATION AND CUSTOMS INSPECTOR: $53,990

INDUSTRIAL MACHINE REPAIRER: $45,000

INSURANCE BROKER: $47,000 to $100,000+

INSURANCE CLAIMS INVESTIGATOR: $58,620

LANDSCAPE FOREMAN: $52,000

LOAN OFFICER: $56,490

MANUFACTURING SALES REPRESENTATIVE: $81,000

MECHANIC: $55,000 (Truck Mechanics can make up to $60,000)

MEDIA EQUIPMENT MANAGER: $61,680

MEDICAL SECRETARY: $51,000

METAL SHOP MACHINE OPERATOR: $49,000

NUCLEAR OPERATOR: $75,600

OCCUPATIONAL THERAPY ASSISTANT: $44,000

ONLINE ADVERTISING MANAGER: $87,000

PEST CONTROL WORKER: $40,340

PERSONAL TRAINER: $30,000 to $70,000

PET GROOMER: $37,000

PHOTOGRAPHER (COMMERCIAL): $76,000

PILE DRIVER OPERATOR: $47,860

PLANT MANAGER: $90,000

PLUMBERS, PIPEFITTERS, AND STEAMFITTERS: $56,660

POLICE AND DETECTIVE SUPERVISOR: $64,430

POSTMASTER: $60,300

POWER PLANT OPERATOR: $63,080

PRODUCTION MANAGER: $74,000

PUMP SYSTEM OPERATOR: $60,040

PURCHASING AGENT: $56,580

RADIATION THERAPIST: $74,900

REAL ESTATE BROKER: $58,720

SALES REPRESENTATIVE (AUTO): $62,000

SALES REPRESENTATIVE (HOME IMPROVEMENT): $85,000

SERVICE TECH (CHEMICAL COMPANY): $55,000

SEWAGE PLANT OPERATOR: $51,000

SKIN-CARE SPECIALIST: $48,920

STORAGE AND DISTRIBUTION MANAGER: $66,600

SUBWAY OR STREETCAR OPERATOR: $57,200

SURVEYOR: $55,000

TELECOMMUNICATIONS EQUIPMENT INSTALLER: $54,710

TRANSPORTATION MANAGER: $77,762

TRUCK DRIVER: $45,000 (for a big-box store: $80,000)

UNITED STATES SENATOR/CONGRESSPERSON: $174,000

TAX COLLECTOR: $54,000

TRADE SHOW MANAGER: $57,000

UNION SHOP STEWARD: $53,000

WAITSTAFF: $40,000 to $70,000

WEB DEVELOPER: $66,000

WEB DESIGNER: $73,300

WELDER: $52,000

WHOLESALE SALES REPRESENTATIVE: $52,000

WRITER: $30,000 to $100,000

SUCCESSFUL PEOPLE WITHOUT COLLEGE DEGREES

If you need more convincing that you don't necessarily have to attend a four-year college or take out an inordinate amount of debt to be successful (and by *successful*, I mean finding comfort, peace, and freedom while following your own unique path), then here is a list of some of the most recognizable folks who "did it their way" and turned out okay. Now, sure, most of these people have made history books or they are millionaires and billionaires, but the reality is, there are millions of folks out there who have managed to create pretty great lives for themselves without a degree. Whenever anyone gives you a hard time for not going to or finishing school, here are some names you can casually drop into the conversation in defense of people who fared pretty well despite never graduating from college:

- **ABRAHAM LINCOLN**—yeah, as in the sixteenth US president. He only finished one year of formal schooling.
- **ANDREW CARNEGIE** is one of the world's most iconic success stories. He was an industrialist and philanthropist, and one of the first megabillionaires in the US. He dropped out of elementary school.
- **ANSEL ADAMS**, a world-famous photographer, dropped out of high school.
- **BENJAMIN FRANKLIN**, one of the forefathers of our country, inventor, and writer, was primarily homeschooled.
- **BILL GATES**, founder of Microsoft and one of the world's richest men, dropped out of college.
- **COCO CHANEL**, the founder of the famed fashion brand Chanel—nope, she didn't get a design degree from Pratt.
- **DAVE THOMAS**, billionaire and founder of Wendy's, dropped out of high school at fifteen.
- **DAVID GEFFEN**, billionaire founder of Geffen Records and cofounder of DreamWorks, completed one year of college.
- **DAVID NEELEMAN**, founder of JetBlue airlines, never graduated from college.
- **DAVID OGILVY**, advertising executive and copywriter, a genius of branding and marketing, was expelled from Oxford University at the age of twenty.
- **FRANK LLOYD WRIGHT**—yes, one of the most influential architects of the twentieth century—never even attended high school, let alone college!
- **GEORGE EASTMAN**, multimillionaire inventor and Kodak founder, dropped out of high school before founding the legendary company.

- **HENRY FORD**, who is the billionaire founder of Ford Motor Company, never attended college.
- **JAMES CAMERON**, Oscar-winning director, screenwriter, and producer, dropped out of college.
- **JOHN D. ROCKEFELLER SR.**, billionaire founder of the Standard Oil Company, dropped out of high school just two months before graduating, though he later took some courses at a local business school.
- **JOHN MACKEY**, founder of Whole Foods, gave it the old college try six times! That's how many times he enrolled and dropped out before founding Whole Foods.
- **KERKOR "KIRK" KERKORIAN**, billionaire investor, owner of Mandalay Bay, The Mirage, and MGM movie studio, dropped out in eighth grade.
- **LARRY ELLISON**, billionaire cofounder of Oracle software company, dropped out of two different colleges.
- **LEANDRO RIZZUTO**, billionaire founder of Conair, dropped out of college and started Conair with $100 and a hot-air hair roller invention.
- **MARY KAY ASH**, founder of Mary Kay Inc., never attended college.
- **MICHAEL DELL**, billionaire founder of Dell, which started out of his college dorm room, eventually dropped out of college.
- **RACHAEL RAY**, Food Network cooking show star and food industry entrepreneur, had NO formal culinary arts training and never went to college.
- **RAY KROC**, legendary CEO of McDonald's, dropped out of high school.
- **RICHARD BRANSON**, the billionaire founder of Virgin

Records, Virgin Atlantic, and Virgin Mobile, and now
author, dropped out of high school at sixteen.

- **SIMON COWELL**, TV producer, music judge, and creator of
  American Idol, *The X Factor*, and *Britain's Got Talent*, is a
  high school dropout.
- **STEVE WOZNIAK**, billionaire cofounder of Apple, did not
  complete college.
- **STEVE JOBS**, innovator and cofounder of Apple, also didn't
  complete college.
- **STEVEN SPIELBERG**, Oscar-winning director and producer,
  dropped out of college.
- **TOM GOLISANO**, founder of Paychex and author of *Built, Not
  Born*, spent two years in a tech school before starting the
  payroll giant with just $3,000. The company currently
  has a market cap of $31 billion.
- **WALT DISNEY**, founder and creative genius behind The Walt
  Disney Company, dropped out of high school at sixteen.

Pretty amazing, huh? I was just as shocked as you when I
put this list together, and it's only a very partial list. So what are
you going to do now?

ABOUT THE AUTHOR

Ken Rusk is a blue-collar construction business entrepreneur who has launched multiple successful endeavors over the last thirty years. In the beginning of his working life, he dug ditches around foundations to fix leaky basements. Over time, he dug his way to a good life, one shovel of dirt at a time, and is teaching others to do the same. Rusk has extensive experience in hiring, training, and developing first-time job seekers, particularly those without college degrees. He lives in Toledo, Ohio, where he runs Rusk Industries, Inc., which specializes in multiple construction endeavors.